Too Smart for God

Pastor Dave Simpson

9FOOT VOICE

www.9footvoice.com

9 Foot Voice - Minnesota

Cover Design by Brittany Kalscheur

ISBN: 978-1-951849-01-6

For Karen, who inspired (and required) me into church,
and got more than she bargained for:
a husband and an Unexpected Pastor.

Contents

Introduction

The Voice of Trebek

I was finally on Jeopardy!

And I was blowing it.

Who Wants to Be Millionaire[i] had been a peak experience, but *Jeopardy!* was the holy grail of game shows.

I stood at the middle podium flanked by returning champion Lowell on my right and fellow challenger Sujit on my left. The bigger-than-I-expected game board towered in front, a repository of unrevealed challenge. Alex Trebek – live and in person! – got the game going.

I knew the correct responses to the first few clues, but kept getting beaten when I tried to ring in. I was determined to be ready for the next one.

The way it works is that you have to wait for Alex to finish reading a clue, then lights around the game board (you can't see them at home) illuminate when the signaling devices are activated. Attempt to ring in too soon and you're locked out for a half-second, an eternity in the fast-moving game.

I waited, and as soon as those lights flashed I furiously mashed the button. Sure enough, the bulbs on top of my podium lit up.

I had rung in first!

"Dave?" Alex said.

---

i. Five years before *Jeopardy!* I sat in the *Millionaire* hot seat across from host Meredith Viera in 2003. I won $125,000 by knowing, among other things, that a Pygmy Marmoset is a tiny monkey and that Kalaallit Nunaat is the indigenous name for Greenland.

Alex Trebek said my name!

But he seemed to be waiting for something. What was it? Oh yeah, I was supposed to give the correct response (in the form of a question).

Here's what I said:

I had focused so much on the timing that I forgot I had to respond. I looked again at the clue – something about a memoir written by a celebrity. A picture of an actress formed in my head, but I couldn't remember her name. (She turned out to be wrong, anyway.)

I stood frozen in panic and watched the five podium lights go out one by one as they counted down the five seconds I had to respond.

I always laughed at people who rang in and then stood there silent and shamed. Now I was one of them.

I recovered. I even went on a streak where I rang in first and correctly responded to the next thirteen clues, including running the "American Revolution" category. I won that game, and then three more, enough to be invited back for the Tournament of Champions where I made it to the semi-finals.

I've been told I am one of three people to have won more than $100,000 on both *Jeopardy!* and *Who Wants to Be a Millionaire*.

This book is not about my game show "career," but I better establish my "Too Smart" cred right away if I'm going to have the audacity to call a book *Too Smart for God*.

I also want to give you a hint of what this book is about:

In the same way I couldn't believe Alex Trebek called my name – and I didn't respond – the first time I rang in on *Jeopardy!*, for much of my life I couldn't believe God had called me. I certainly didn't have a response.

Unlike Alex Trebek, who was standing right there and whose reality was undeniable, I didn't believe God even existed.

I am an Unexpected Pastor.

I am surprised even to be a Christian.

This book is about how I came to hear God's voice and finally to respond.

Our Journey Begins

1

It's All Connected

Smart folks can be Christians and Christians can be smart folks.

It would be easy to blame "the media" for the popular conception of Christians as dumber than dirt, but we followers of Jesus shoulder much of the blame.

We keep sending our money to TV preachers who give simplistic answers to questions like, "Why do terrible things happen?"

Their answers usually revolve around God punishing people those TV preachers happen to hate (LGBTQ folks seem to provoke hurricanes), and who aren't in the donor database.

We Christians keep sharing shallow memes promising prosperity and popularity if you just believe enough . . . and share the memes. God wants you to live a "blessed" life, which means rich and famous.

That works out well for the rich and famous prosperity preachers.

The rest of us – Christians in general – look gullible and stupid because we fall for the same empty promises and shallow theology over and over again. I understand the desire for hope, but only false hope can be found in guarantees of a problem-free life.

———

One of the primary reasons I came to believe Christianity is true[i] is that it describes the world as it really is: messed up, often disappointing, hurtful and inconstant, but at the same time abounding in poten-

i. Finding truth in Christianity is different than believing every assertion and event in the Bible is factually correct.

tial for love and joy.

Even more than that, I believe Christianity is true because it describes people as they really are: messed up, often disappointing, hurtful and inconstant, but at the same time abounding in potential for love and joy.

Most of all, I believe Christianity is true because it describes me as I really am: messed up and . . . you know the rest.

———

Beware preachers spewing easy answers.

Christianity ain't *Jeopardy!* or even *Who Wants to Be a Millionaire.*

I made a lot of money knowing the answers.

Since I realized I was a Christian, and especially since I've been a pastor, I've learned I don't need to know all the answers, or even many of them.

In real life, "I don't know" is often the smartest thing I can say.

———

If I don't know all the answers, you might wonder what's in this book.

Here's my strongest argument for reading *Too Smart for God*:

IT'S NOT ABOUT ME.

Rick Warren sold millions of copies of *The Purpose Driven Life*, a book that started with this sentence:

"It's not about you."

I'm not just ripping off Rick Warren.

This book really is not about me.

"Wait a minute, Dave," you might protest. "Isn't this your story? How can you say this book is not about you?!"

Because this book is about God.

A pretty bold claim, but I mean it with the deepest humility. My life is the vehicle by which we will take this journey.

And God, to continue this classic but effective metaphor, is the operator of that vehicle.

You may have seen this bumper sticker:

"GOD IS MY CO-PILOT."

There's another one I prefer:

"IF GOD IS YOUR CO-PILOT, YOU'RE IN THE WRONG SEAT."

It is only by looking back that I can see how Jesus did indeed . . . take the wheel.

(Deepest apologies to Carrie Underwood.[ii])

———

Don't get me wrong.

I'm not saying everything in my life, especially my choices, was determined and manipulated by God.

God is not Jim Henson.

I am not Kermit. Or even Fozzie Bear.

God is not some cosmic puppeteer pulling our strings or even a divine director guiding us through a tragic script.

I once experienced a car accident that resulted in a lot of pain, but ultimately strengthened my faith. I do not believe God grabbed hold of the other car, pulled it through a red light and smashed it broadside into mine like a child playing with Matchbox cars on their bedroom floor.

No, God didn't cause the accident.

Too Smart for God is not a story of how I came back to God, because God was always there – before, during and after my accident.

God was always here.

God is always here.

God is here in these pages.

One of my favorite films is *The World According to Garp*, based on one of my favorite books by John Irving. In the film, the title character, played by Robin Williams, says, "It's really nice, you know, to look back and see the arc of your life, and it's all connected. How you got from there to here. To see the lines."

This is what I see as I look back over the arc of my life:

God used the story of my life to write God's story in me.

———

ii. Carrie Underwood is another game show contestant. My bud. Not really. Never met her. But we do have that in common. She won Season Four of American Idol, and one of her biggest hits was "Jesus Take the Wheel." Most of you knew that, but folks reading the Buryat translation of this book in Mongolia will need the help.

2

You Can Be Cleopas

The Protypical Christian Conversion Story in the Bible involves a man named Saul who literally saw the light. When we meet Saul in the Book of Acts[i] he is a devout Jew but a despicable person. He hates Christians (which doesn't in itself make him despicable). Saul considers them apostates – threats to his faith - who are multiplying like rats ever since their leader died and supposedly came back to life three days later.

Saul puts his enmity into action. At the stoning of Stephen,[ii] the first Christian martyr, Saul didn't have the guts to partake in the actual execution. Instead, he held the coats of those who hurled the fatal rocks.

There is something particularly smarmy about that kind of "I don't want to get my hands dirty" participation in a murderous mob.

In the ninth chapter of Acts, Saul is on his way to the Syrian city of Damascus. He is "breathing murderous threats against" followers of Jesus.

Christians really piss him off.

At Saul's request, the authorities have given him a mandate to

---

i. Acts is a New Testament book. It's the first book after the four Gospels that tell the story of Jesus' life, death, and resurrection. The full name of the book is "The Acts of the Apostles." It follows Jesus' disciples (or apostles) as they spread the Good News about Jesus all over the Roman Empire, often at the cost of their freedom or even their lives. It reads sort of like a novel, with gruesome executions, ship wrecks, and dynamic personalities, including Saul/Paul.

ii. Death by throwing stones, not the use of mind-altering substances.

round up Damascus Christians and imprison them. Saul is portrayed as such a vile villain that when I read this story I picture him twirling his mustache and rubbing his hands with glee as he nears Damascus.

But then! A brilliant light flashes from heaven, so bright it instantly blinds Saul. A voice says, "Saul, Saul, why are you persecuting me?"

It's Jesus!

Saul gets the point, and after a Christian restores his sight Saul becomes the greatest evangelist of the New Testament – and maybe ever.

Even bigger than Billy Graham!

Like many others in the Bible (and many modern celebrities), his name got changed.

He became, "The Apostle Formerly Known as Saul."

His name was written as an indecipherable symbol.

No, sorry.

That was Prince.

Saul was hereafter known as Paul.

———

Now that's a great story!

My story is not quite like that.

I was not a man of faith before I became a Christian.

I didn't kill Christians. I just made fun of them.

I was never blinded by a heavenly light.

Jesus never personally rebuked me.

If any of that ever happened, this would be a much shorter book.

———

My story is different from most others who write books in the Spiritual Conversion genre.

I didn't do a lot of the dramatic and (self-) destructive things they recount.

I drank too much, but I wasn't an alcoholic or a drug addict.

I've been divorced and I've lived with a woman who's not my wife, but my sexual exploits were pretty tame compared to, say, King Solomon.[iii]

I don't have a tale of child abuse and/or neglect; my family had its quirks, but we weren't dramatically dysfunctional.

---

iii. According to the Bible, King Solomon had 700 wives and 300 concubines.

I suspect my story is more common than instantaneous conversions like Paul's.

My story is more like the other great conversion story in the Bible, the one that happened not on the Road to Damascus but rather on the Road to Emmaus . . .

———

Luke tells the story in Chapter 24 of his Gospel.[iv] It happens on the first Easter Sunday.

Jesus died two days before.

Two of Jesus' followers – Cleopas and one who is not named, so I'll call him "Dave" – have just left Jerusalem. They are walking toward Emmaus, a town a few miles away.

Cleopas and Dave's journey is symbolic of their emotional and spiritual state. Jerusalem was the city of hope, the city where the Hebrew Scriptures promised the Savior would conquer and establish a perfectly just rule over the world. Cleopas and Dave, along with many who followed Jesus, believed Jesus to be that Savior.

But then they saw him nailed to a cross where he died just like any other man.

That wasn't what the Savior was supposed to do!

So Cleopas and Dave walked away from Jerusalem. Away from hope. Away from faith.

Cleopas and Dave were at the end of their hope.

As they walk, they discuss the events of the last few days. Another traveler joins them along the way. Luke tells us in an aside that this newcomer is the resurrected Jesus, but Cleopas and Dave don't recognize him.

Jesus asks why they are so sad.

They can't believe their new companion hasn't heard what happened to Jesus. Cleopas and Dave tell him the whole story.

Jesus gets angry. "Don't you get it?! Don't you know the Scriptures?! Dying and rising again was what the Savior was supposed to do all along."

———

iv. The Gospels – Matthew, Mark, Luke, and John – begin the New Testament. Each tells the story of the life, death, and resurrection of Jesus from a slightly different perspective. My favorite is Luke, but if you haven't read them yet you might want to start with Mark. It's the shortest.

Then Jesus teaches them sort of a Sunday School lesson about how the promises in the Hebrew Scriptures were about, well . . . him.

They talk until it's time to stop for dinner. Cleopas and Dave sit down. They invite Jesus to eat with them. A meal is laid out.

Jesus picks up some bread, breaks it, and blesses it.

Light bulbs appear.

This is Jesus!

This is the Savior they'd been waiting for!

Because he didn't fit their idea of what the Savior should be, they gave up on him. They rejected him.

Cleopas and Dave walked away from their faith.

But Jesus was walking with them all along.

Luke goes on to tell us that Cleopas and Dave ran back to Jerusalem and told everyone their story of walking with Jesus, of finding him – and their faith – even though they didn't know they were looking for him – or for it.

And that, my new friend, is what I will do in the rest of this book.

I will tell you how I walked away from my faith because God and Jesus didn't meet my expectations . . . and didn't answer all my smart-guy questions.

I'll show you how Jesus walked with me even when I didn't recognize him, much less believe him to be my (or anyone else's) Savior.

Finally, you'll see how I realized, not in a flash but over the course of the walk, who Jesus is not just for the world but for me.

Like Cleopas and Dave, I can't help but tell the world about it.

―――

That's where we're headed on this journey together.

I'll be Dave.

You can be Cleopas.

3

A Caveat

WARNING – I love learning useless information.[i] There are plenty of digressions in this book where I indulge that avocation.

In fact, one title I considered was *Digressions*, sort of a play on *Confessions*[ii].

In order to keep some semblance of a flow, I put the most extraneous trivia into footnotes you can ignore or not. They are mostly factoids[iii] I picked up or was reminded of while writing this book. The information might be interesting to you or it might make you feel smart when you say, "I already knew that."

It is also knowledge you can monetize should you ever find yourself on a game show.

Another thing about the footnotes.

I am not assuming everyone who reads *Too Smart for God* is familiar with the basics of Christian faith. As you've seen, there will

---

i. The Move, a '60s British rock band that begat ELO, had a song called "Useless Information." I am now listening to it, having looked it up on YouTube. Detours like this are a big reason this book took so long to write.

ii. The most famous *Confessions* was by St. Augustine, but others have written them in the 1600 or so years since. Which reminds me: St. Augustine, Florida, is the oldest city in the United States. But don't pronounce St. Augustine the saint like St. Augustine the city. (See, this book has already been worth what you paid for it in saving you that embarrassment.)

iii. The word "factoid" was created by Norman Mailer in his Marilyn Monroe biography. That is a factoid factoid.

be occasional footnotes explaining foundational matters.

If you already know that stuff, it's another opportunity to feel superior.

4

My Major Misconception (Amazing Grace 1)

When I was an unChristian, my biggest misunderstanding about Christianity was this:

Christians are people who run around trying to obey the Ten Commandments and other rules *so that* God will love them and let them into heaven.

This is what I know now that I am a Christian:

Christians are people who run around trying to follow the Ten Commandments and other rules *because* God loves us and God already promised us eternity.

We try to love God and love our neighbors not in order to get something, but because we already have . . . Everything.

This is what you have to do to be a Christian:

Nothing.[i]

God – in Jesus – has already done it all for us.

That is grace.

Grace is God's undeserved gift of love, forgiveness, and salvation.

Grace changed my life.

We're going to pause for a moment so I can tell you how I have come to understand grace, otherwise my journey won't make any sense.

Grace is the force that propelled this story even – especially – when

---

i. This is too radical even for some Christians. A church near mine put that on their sign: "What do you need to do to be saved? Nothing." The pastor got angry phone calls from CHRISTIANS who were offended by God's grace. So of course I had to put it on my church's sign . . .

12

I didn't realize it.

I'm not writing about grace in order to convince you of its reality.

This is not the equivalent of a pitch to become my Amway multi-level marketing minion in the middle of a nice dinner I invited you to.

It's like this: If I were writing a science fiction novel, I'd want you to have an idea of how the spaceships are powered. You wouldn't have to completely understand or even agree that this motive force[ii] was possible in the real world. But you'd need to know something about it for the story to make sense.

And that, my friend, is probably the nerdiest spiritual metaphor you will ever read.

Let's get back to grace . . .

Remember Paul? Paul the Evangelist[iii] formerly known as Saul the Persecutor of Christians? Paul once wrote a letter to the church in Galatia[iv] to set folks straight who wanted to make Christianity all about the rules.

Follow the rules and then God will love you, they said.

Follow the rules and then God will forgive you, they said.

Follow the rules and then Jesus will save you, they said.

Paul said: Spoiler alert! Jesus didn't wait for you to follow the rules. He died while we were still disobedient.[v]

Christians in Paul's time – and Christians today – wanted to make faith into a sort of math equation.

Jesus' Good Work + Our Good Work = Salvation

It makes logical sense, I guess, but God isn't bound by our ideas of logic and sense.

In another letter Paul wrote,[vi] he said the Gospel – the good news about Jesus – is "foolishness" to the world.

God is countercultural. You can see that in Jesus – God in human skin. Jesus was so countercultural the guardians of culture nailed him

---

ii. *Motive force* is a scientific term for a cause or origin of movement.

iii. *Evangelism* is from the Greek word for the announcement of victory after a battle. For Christians, it is the sharing of Christ's victory over death at the cross and empty tomb.

iv. The book of Galatians was written to the church in Galatia, a city in what was called Asia Minor in the First Century, but we know as Turkey today.

v. Romans 5:8

vi. First Corinthians

to a cross and killed him.

Paul knew those folks obsessed with rules had it backwards. Obedience doesn't earn salvation.

You obey because you are saved.

God always moves first.

How did Paul know God always moves first?

From his own experience.

Remember, God didn't wait for Paul to get his life together before claiming him. When Jesus showed up, Paul was on his way to Damascus to throw Christians in jail.

Jesus showed up anyway.

God loved Paul anyway.

Even though Paul was - as he calls himself in another of his letters - The Chief of Sinners.[vii]

Paul went on to travel around the Roman world telling others this good news: God loves us so much that God became one of us and even died.

God didn't do that because we deserve it.

God did that because God loves us.

That's GRACE.

That's the word that changed my life.

vii. I Timothy 1:15

Virginia

5

Crybabies

My earliest memory takes place in the basement of a church. I'm held by a lady in a black dress. I can't stop crying. I think I'm screaming. I must have been three. It was time to move out of the nursery where infants and toddlers played, pooped, peed, and napped with blissful contentment during the Sunday School hour.

This was the day I joined the big boys and girls in Real Sunday School.

But I didn't want to leave.

I liked it there in that safe cocoon of no expectations. I wanted to stay in the protective arms of the lady in the black dress, the Nursery Lady in whose lap I was bawling. I held onto her with everything my three-year-old self could muster.

I don't remember who was trying to get me to leave. It might have been my parents or some church authority. All I can recall is that black dress the Nursery Lady was wearing, and my emotional cocktail: the desire to stay, shaken with the stark terror of the unknown.

I would do a lot of crying about church as I grew up, mostly about having to go. It was never my idea of the way to spend a Sunday morning. If my parents were still around, I would ask them if I cried during my baptism on June 21, 1963, at Tuckahoe Presbyterian Church in Richmond, Virginia.[i] My guess is that I did.

---

i. Presbyterians – and Lutherans, and most other mainline protestant denominations, plus Roman Catholics - practice infant baptism. Baptists and other more fundamentalist denominations only baptize those who are able to decide they want to be baptized.

As a pastor now one of the best things I get to do is to baptize babies (as well as youth and adults). Often infants will bust out wailing as I pour water over their little bald heads three times – in the name of the Father, and of the Son, and of the Holy Spirit.

Parents are often embarrassed by the tears. "He's usually so good," they say, whatever that means for an infant.

But I think of babies crying as, well, normal. Especially as a response to baptism. The people you trust most in the world – your parents – lift you up in front of a crowd and let some strange man or woman throw water on your head; crying seems sensible, especially when you don't have the words to express, "What are you doing to me?"

Plus, a baby crying in baptism will preach![ii]

Lutherans (and other denominations that practice infant baptism) believe stuff happens in baptism.

Or more exactly, God does actual stuff in baptism.

In baptism, God claims a person, regardless of age, as God's child.

Baptism is God's adoption.

When I met Philip, he was three years old. A year after that first meeting, I married his mom, Karen. Philip became my stepson.

When he was ten, we went to court. I sat in the witness stand and the judge asked, "Why do you want to adopt Philip?"

I considered lots of practical answers. Because I can provide for him. Because I can raise him right. Because we've already lived together for six years.

But in the end, I chose to tell the judge the most true and important reason I wanted to adopt Philip.

"Because I love him."

That's what happens in baptism!

God says, "Because I love you, you are my child."

God's love does not need to be earned. It cannot be earned.

God's love is. God is love.

That's all wonderful, but there is a part of us – our very nature, our very human nature – that doesn't want to be adopted by God.

We can't stand unconditional love.

Even though we don't have to do anything to earn God's love, being

---

ii. Not literally. Although we baptize infants in the Lutheran church, we don't allow them to preach. To say something "will preach" means it will work well in a sermon.

loved calls us to respond. We are commissioned to love as we are loved:

Unconditionally and sacrificially.

But we resist.

We want to love conditionally. And who wants to sacrifice?

A baby crying in baptism provides an excellent metaphor for our resistance to God's love.

Like I said, that wailing infant will preach.

———

On June 21, 1963, God adopted me. God promised to always be with me, to never reject me.

Even if I rejected God.

Which I did.

I did not abandon my faith and become an unChristian[iii] because I didn't like feeling obligated to love unconditionally and sacrificially.

I didn't even know that was part of the deal.

I thought all Christian rules started, "Thou shalt not!"

And ended with some variation of, "Have any fun."

I didn't leave Christianity because of the rules. (Although certainly the emphasis on supposed rules that affect people-not-like-us turned me off.)

I abandoned Christianity because I thought the whole God and Jesus thing was bullshit.

To paraphrase the title, I was Too Smart for That Bullshit[iv].

I'm making this point for my brothers and sisters in the church who think atheists and agnostics aren't Christians because "They don't want anybody telling them what to do."

Sure they don't. NONE OF US wants anybody telling us what to do. That's our human nature.

———

iii. I'll use "unChristian" throughout the book. It is inclusive of those who identify with religions other than Christianity or no religion at all, and is a good descriptor of my unaffiliated spiritual status that oscillated on a continuum between ambivalent agnosticism and absolute atheism.

iv. You're thinking, "But Dave didn't have the guts to name his book *Too Smart for That Bullshit*." And you're right! I barely have the guts to include profanity in this book at all, but I'm writing about stuff with strong emotional resonance and sometimes need words with that kind of heft. Maybe if we sell a lot of books I can do what rappers do and publish a "clean" version. Which is perhaps the only time you'll ever see me write the phrase, "I can do what rappers do." I am not anywhere near that poetic or musically artistic.

I had Christians tell me when I confessed my unbelief, "Oh, you just like doing your own thing."[v]

Where does the conversation go from there?

I don't pray for my unChristian friends to know God is the boss. Or that I'm right and they're wrong.

I pray they will know how much God loves them.

Unconditionally.

Sacrificially.

Because that is the most important, most wonderful thing I know.

———

Speaking of babies crying (which we were a couple pages ago), I think the most ridiculous words ever in a Christmas song are these from "Away in a Manger":

"The little Lord Jesus, no crying he makes."

That one line totally negates the miracle of the incarnation – God in human flesh. Jesus was fully human as well as fully God.[vi]

When Jesus was born he was therefore fully baby. (And fully God.)

Of course he cried!

How else could he tell Mary and Joseph he was cold, hungry,[vii] or thirsty . . . or he needed his diaper changed?

Yeah, fully human baby Jesus filled his diaper.

Some people aren't comfortable talking about the bodily functions of the Savior, so we sing foolishness like, "No crying he makes," or even invent heretical theologies in which Jesus' humanity was just an illusion.[viii]

---

v. I wrote this book first to my UnChristian self. You might, therefore, want to give it to someone who reminds you of me. If you've said these things to them, please deliver an apology along with the book. More about that in Chapter 40, "How to Chase Away an UnChristian."

vi. Don't think about this dual nature of Christ too much; it will make your head hurt. This is true of the Trinity as well. Faith, as I have come to understand, means not having everything figured out.

vii. Mary nursed the baby Jesus, which makes ridiculous the hang ups folks have about women breastfeeding. Please know you are welcome to breastfeed in the church I serve. What a wonderful picture of love!

viii Docetism is the fancy theological word for this heresy. The Nicene Creed in 325 AD was the Christian church's NO to this idea that Jesus wasn't fully human, he just appeared that way. But sometimes we Christians still emphasize the divinity of Jesus so much that we forget the miracle of his humanity – the incarnation, God in the flesh (not to be confused

One of the best things I ever heard a pastor say changed my whole attitude about kids crying not just in church but in other public places like restaurants. Pastor Calvin (real name) said he used to get mad when a baby started wailing and interrupted his meal or whatever, but then he remembered Jesus had been a baby and had most certainly cried.

From then on, every time he heard a baby bawling he thought, "Jesus is here." And he was never annoyed or angry again.

At least about that.

———

Getting back to my baptism (I warned you earlier this book could have been called *Digressions*) . . .

Like I said I would guess I was a crier. Based on my childhood-long resistance to church, I'd be surprised if I didn't put up a fight as God claimed me in those baptismal waters.

I'd also like to ask my parents why they waited over a year after I was born to get me baptized. Why wasn't my baptism more of a priority when church seemed so all-fired important when I was growing up?

But that's not entirely accurate. Church was important . . . on Sundays. The Simpsons were faithfully in Sunday School, then the pews for worship every week.

But I don't remember a lot of (any?) conversations about Jesus or God or the Bible on other days. I have a dim recollection of bedtime stories from a picture Bible when I was very young, but other than that I don't recall anyone picking up any kind of Bible or reading it.

I'm not implying, "And that's why I walked away from the church and from God." It's not that simple, and it's no one's fault but my own.

Besides, for the most part I had an awesome childhood.

———

with "In the Flesh," a song from My Favorite Album Ever: Pink Floyd's *The Wall*.)

6

Happy Little Simpsons

My mother was a stay-home mom from the time I was born through my elementary school years. We were an unremarkably normal nuclear family unit: a mom, a dad, me, a sister two years younger, two cats, one dog. Until I was twelve, we lived in a three-bedroom brick house in Henrico County outside of Richmond, Virginia.

When I go back and look at that home on Gardenia Drive,[i] I can't believe there are three bedrooms in the barely cabin-sized dwelling. It is dwarfed by much larger split-levels on either side. But it never seemed small when we lived there.

The idyllic nature of my early childhood is at the heart of the little song my mom made up with my sister and me as we sat on the front porch one day. Woodman Terrace was the name of our neighborhood. If you'd like to sing along, the tune is the same as "Frère Jacques" which is also known as "Are You Sleeping" and which has the same melody as "Where Is Thumbkin":[ii]

Woodman Terrace, Woodman Terrace
We live here, we live here

---

i. Do you remember your childhood address? How about your phone number? I remember facts, but numbers usually don't stick as well. But not only did I not have to look up the address, my Gardenia Drive phone number is embedded in my memory – 266-5391.

ii. Did you realize "Mary Had a Little Lamb" has the same tune as "London Bridge"? Or that "The Alphabet Song" is just "Mary Had a Little Lamb" with letters substituted for the words? Or that Barney's "I Love You" ripped off "This Old Man" for its tune? These are more good things to know if you're ever on a game show.

Happy little Simpsons, happy little Simpsons
Ha ha ha, ha ha ha

Kind of catchy, huh?

My mom was no Tim Rice[iii], or even Raffi[iv], but the simplicity of the lyrics encapsulates the timbre of my early childhood. Woodman Terrace was a community in the late '60s and early '70s where kids stayed out late in the summer playing hide and seek with no regard to property lines.

City kids had to come in when the street lights came on.

We didn't have street lights in the suburbs.

I don't remember any "Get off my lawn!" kind of neighbors, although we were supposed to stay out of the backyard next door because there was an in-ground pool where you could drown. But I retrieved many Wiffle Ball home runs over there.

And I never drowned.

Everyone's mom watched out for every kid, and didn't feel shy about correcting them, either. You were supposed to stay out of "The Woods," a few undeveloped acres between the community and the Safeway Shopping Center, because "Hippies" hung out there.

But that didn't stop us from building forts along the periphery.

Just sleeping out in the back yard in the bright yellow tent with a blue cowboy drawn on the side felt like a big adventure. It got DARK at night.

Church was what everybody did on Sundays. "The Catholics" who lived behind us ("That's why they have so many kids") and the Protestants all around. One time I heard something on a news program my father was watching about the Troubles in Northern Ireland and wondered if our Catholic neighbors were mad at us, but other than that religion was never a source of conflict or even conversation.

---

iii. Tim Rice is the awesome lyricist who collaborated with Andrew Lloyd Webber on Broadway hits like *Jesus Christ Superstar* and *Evita*, and later with Elton John on *The Lion King*. But his best work, in my opinion, was with former ABBA members on the underappreciated musical, *Chess*.

iv. Raffi is best known for his children's music, especially "Baby Beluga" and "Bananaphone." In the late 80's when I managed a record store, he was the go-to artist for kids songs. His first four albums were engineered by Daniel Lanois, who later produced albums by such superstars as Peter Gabriel, U2, and Bob Dylan.

God was an old (white) guy who'd probably moved to the suburbs along with everyone else – at least all the white people – and who expected us to listen to our parents and be nice.

There were few people of color in our lives. The only African-American person I can ever remember seeing in Woodman Terrace was a maid who took care of the house and watched a friend of mine during the day. What stands out for me about her in the hindsight of memory is that he introduced her as "Mary" in a culture of southern formality where children were expected to address adults as "Mr. Smith" and "Mrs. Jones."

I went to school in Henrico County through the sixth grade; in all that time I had exactly one classmate of color. He only stayed for half a year, but not because he was pressured to leave. I remember tears rolling down his cheeks when he transferred out because he didn't want to go.

For individuals, often even those who are "different," many Southerners cloak their insularity in hospitality.

It is groups of "others" who provoke discomfort.

And hatred.

One day in third grade my mom kept my sister and me home from school as part of a boycott to protest a talked-about (but never implemented) plan to integrate Henrico County Schools by merging with the Richmond City District. Not that my mom was any kind of segregationist rabble rouser.

It was me who begged her to let me take the day off.

It seemed kind of like a snow day.

At first my mom insisted we go to school. But then she started calling other parents and only agreed to the day off when she made sure other kids were boycotting also.

"What everyone else is doing" and "What will everyone else think?" were crucial moral determinates for my mom. I don't blame her, though.

It was a conformist culture, especially for women.

It turned out the kids who did go to school that day got free ice cream and played games, so I ended up regretting my "snow day."

It was a lesson in political activism.

There's always a price.

Especially in Safe, Segregated, Southern Suburbia.

7

Doing Time in the Big
House (of God)

Church was even more monochromatic than school.

I do not remember encountering a person of color in any of the churches we attended when I was growing up.

Unfortunately, Reverend King's[i] observation in a 1960 *Meet the Press* interview was accurate then, and continues to be accurate now:

"I think it a tragedy in our nation, one of the shameful tragedies, that eleven o'clock on Sunday morning is one of the most segregated hours, if not the most segregated hour, in America."

By the time I entered kindergarten, we had transferred to Lakeside Presbyterian. It was a picturesque little brick church with a tall white steeple reaching up to heaven. The congregation must have been a healthy size because we had two pastors, Mr. Boyce and Mr. McGirt (attempts at their real names, but probably botched spelling).

I liked when Mr. McGirt preached because he would often illustrate his sermons with descriptions of scenes from movies, mostly ones I wasn't allowed to see.

Lakeside Presbyterian was a safe place to spend our Sundays.

I no longer believe church is supposed to be so safe. Physically secure, of course, but not safe from challenge by new and different ideas – and especially people.

Sunday School was its own separate space where felt cutouts of fro-

---

i. Dr. Martin Luther King Jr. was first and foremost a minister of the Gospel, most famously at Ebenezer Baptist Church in Atlanta. The Bible's principles of justice and liberation underpinned all of his civil rights work. I did not learn that at the churches in which I grew up.

zen-faced caucasian Bible characters cavorted on flannelboards, manipulated by sweet southern ladies whose hair and makeup were, like my mom's, "Just so." And who, also like my mom, would protest if you hugged them too tight: "Don't mess me up!"

At least we got cookies and juice!

It was in church that I first found a use for multiplication. The church service itself wasn't what you would call kid-friendly. In those days there weren't Children's Sermons or Busy Bags or Coloring Pages or any of the other distractions for young people you find now. No, we had to sit up straight and not wrinkle our Sunday Clothes. To do otherwise would make our parents look bad and earn a sour disapproving stare from one of the Church Ladies in their regular seats (hell hath no fury like a Church Lady whose seat has been swiped) who presided over the pews and assured proper decorum.

I got the impression God was kind of like the cranky old fellows who hobbled into church each Sunday and sat up front except when it was their turn to usher. They smelled of mildew and cigarettes and wanted kids to be seen and not heard.

They didn't seem too sure about the "seen" part.

On some Sundays, well, on most Sundays, church seemed to last FOREVER.

Eternity was a concept grasped experientially by regular church attendance.

I have always had trouble sitting still and would fidget a lot – and get lots of shushes from my mom and even some, "We'll deal with this later" looks from my dad up in the choir loft where he sang tenor.

I would just wonder why we had to spend the longest hour of the week sitting in the hardest seat imaginable wearing the most uncomfortable clothes we owned. I spent a lot of time daydreaming, telling myself stories of heroism featuring me in the leading role, with soundtracks provided by the pipe organ.

I did pay attention to the worship bulletin[ii]. The first thing I would do when we got to our seats in a pew toward the front – but not too

---

ii. The bulletin is like the program for church. It lists the order in which everything happens in the service including the Scripture readings and sermon title. Plus there are usually announcements in case you want to know when the Youth are having their next bake sale or that the Sunday School is in desperate need of teachers again.

close – was open up the bulletin to see which creed we were saying that week. Seeing the relatively short Apostle's Creed listed was always a bonus compared to the interminable (and unintelligible: "begotten, not made, being of one substance with the Father," what??) Nicene Creed.

Then I would take out a hymnal from the rack on the back of the pew in front of us and look up the hymns for the day. I remember how the hymnal felt softer than normal paper, tenderized by years and years of parishioners turning the pages. I was very discerning about which hymns I liked and which I didn't. I had a very objective system.

That's where multiplication came in.

After I learned to multiply in third grade, I would rate each hymn based on the number of verses times the number of lines. A three-line hymn may look shorter on the page than a four-line one, but not if it had six verses and the four-line one had only four.

It only got worse when I got a watch and could time the various parts of the service.

Church proved the Theory of Relativity. Time moved at a different, much slower speed in church than it did everywhere else.

Don't get me wrong. Lakeside Presbyterian nurtured me and the other kids who grew up in the congregation. I was only twelve when we left Virginia. I did not recognize most deficiencies outlined in these chapters until I got older.

But even as a pre-teen forced-faithful attender, I sensed what happened in church on Sundays didn't resonate much the rest of the week. We worshiped in the "sanctuary." The sanctuary walls protected God's people from the outside world. Those walls also kept God – or God's people – from influencing the outside world too much.

God dwelt there in "God's house." Did that mean God could only be found under the steeple, or that God was somehow less present elsewhere?

We kept God in God's place, mostly in church but otherwise in safe and expected territory. We prayed at home before meals, but never in restaurants.

I guess God didn't want us embarrassing ourselves.

We were also expected to pray before bed.

My nightly prayer ritual began with a recitation of "Now I lay me down to sleep . . ." including those always comforting words for young children, "And if I die before I wake, I pray the Lord my soul to take."

No wonder I had nightmares.

Then I would do my very own blessing prayer. "God bless Mommy, God bless Daddy, God bless Anne (my sister), God bless Grandma," and so on. The blessed lined up in the same order every night. I'm sure I found comfort in the routine but I also didn't want to accidentally miss anybody. Who knows what would happen if I forgot to bless some relative or other.

I wouldn't want that guilt on my hands!

God seemed a lot like the school bully.

You needed to appease God to keep God from pummeling you.

Occasionally you had to give up your dessert to the bully.

What kept the plagues and smiting at bay was prayer, listening to your mom and dad, and especially giving God that hour or two a week at Lakeside Presbyterian.

8

The Rolling Tones

During elementary school I sang in the Cherub Choir. The coolest part of that group was the white robes we wore on the rare occasions they let us sing in "big church."

If you pulled the collar up over your head, those robes made you into a mighty fine ghost!

The Choir Director, a tightly wound woman who was more suited to working with professionals than snotty elementary schoolers, somehow failed to appreciate the cool factor and demanded we, "Wear those robes correctly or you won't wear anything at all."

I think she meant no robes.

I hope so.

Christmas Eve service my third grade year was going to be exciting because the Cherub Choir was going to put on those robes and sing TWO songs!

One was "Silent Night." All I remember about that one is the choir director's apoplexy over our making "peace" in the first "Sleep in heavenly peace" a big slur of notes rather than making a smooth transition between the syllables. She wanted "Peeee-eeeece." We kept giving her "Peeeeeeeeece" with the "ee's" climbing, climbing, climbing ever higher like a screeching Jacob's ladder.

But the biggest burr under the choir director's piano bench was the "Pa rum pum pum pum's" in "The Little Drummer Boy." She wanted us to "rrrroll those rrrr's" each time we said "rum."

"Pa rrrrum pum pum pum" is the effect she wanted. It was very important to her.

I don't remember her name, but I remember the choir director rolling her own rrrr's to demonstrate over and over as if Mary might not nod and Jesus might not smile[i] if we didn't get it right.

Or as if our eternal salvation – and hers – depended on the proper rolling of rrrr's.

But I was lost. You see, if I had been born in Mexico or some other Spanish-speaking country, I would have been thrown into speech therapy. It is impossible for me to roll my Rs. I've tried . . . Lord knows I've tried and never harder than in the Cherub Choir in third grade. But my tongue just will not cooperate. (I just tried again. Darn you, tongue!)

One afternoon at rehearsal as Christmas drew near the choir director winced with each "Pa rum pum pum pum." I thought I could just blend in, but her trained ear was having none of it.

"Who is not rolling their rrrr's?"

Crickets.

"I'll have each one of you sing it solo. Speak up now."

What could I do? I raised my chubby hand, the Shame of the Cherub Choir.

"Well, you just mouth the words to this one, David."

"All of them, or just the 'Pa rum pum pum pums?"

She flinched again at my flat *rum*. "All of them. The entire song. It won't do for you to be jumping in and out like a jack-in-the-box."

So on Christmas Eve I stood there with the other kids in my white robe facing the congregation, doing my best not to slur the notes on "Silent Night," then being Milli or Vanilli[ii] on "The Little Drummer Boy."

---

i. In the song, in response to the Little Drummer Boy's drumming, Mary nods and the baby Jesus smiles. It seems the last thing a brand new mom would want would be a kid banging on a drum. And a smile would perhaps be the least likely response from a baby.

ii. Of course this was 1971, long before "Girl You Know It's True" [That We Can't Sing]. For you young folks, Milli Vanilli had a huge hit with that song in 1989, and even won a Grammy Award for Best New Artist. It was later revealed that neither Milli nor Vanilli sang on the record – or on stage. Everything was lip-synched. At the time I was managing a record store, and one of the writers of the song came in every week to check out its position on the Billboard Charts. A brush with fame!

It's crazy, but as I write this I can still experience that "everybody's looking at me, the kid who can't roll an R" feeling. I don't need to look into the mirror to see that my cheeks are turning crimson. I was letting down the Choir Director, the pastors, and probably God Himself. (God was most definitely a "Him" in those days.)

The church has historically been clueless about folks who do not conform.

I was going to write "the church has struggled" with folks who do not conform, but that would imply effort.

Conformist flaccidity characterizes many American churches, including the ones in which I grew up.

When I thought of church, especially during my time as an unChristian, I pictured white middle-class straight male-dominant congregations. The ranks of unChristians are full of folks who don't quite conform to the norm and have been hurt by churches and church people.

Churches accomplish the opposite of evangelism when they make folks who are different feel awful about themselves . . . and persuade them to believe God's overwhelming attitude toward them is disappointment.

All in the name of Jesus!

Amen!

Church standards often have as much to do with cultural norms as they do theological principles. Those who do not conform have been, and still are in many congregations, encouraged to straighten up or leave (more literally for LGBTQ folks).

Because being "nice" is one of the most important of those norms, pressure to conform typically takes passive-aggressive forms. When confronted, shunning is excused as obliviousness: "I didn't see you there!" The sharp edges of cutting comments are sheathed with wiggle room for deniability: "I didn't mean anything by it!" Ultimately, it is the target's fault: "You're awfully sensitive!"

Some churches and Christians are fluent in weaponized love.

You know you're about to be walloped by a Christian when they tell you they are going to "Speak the truth in love."

If that's love, the J. Geils band was right.

"Love Stinks."[iii]

Perhaps worst of all, nonconformists are bashed while the assailant claims, "I'm just hating the sin and loving the sinner."

It sounds so theological. So caring.

So nice.

"Hate the sin and love the sinner" is nowhere in the Bible. But Good Christian Folks think it is commanded in Holy Scripture and therefore believe they have license to treat people like crap who commit the "sins" they prioritize as the worst.

You know, the "sins" they don't struggle with themselves.

Or that secretly torment them.

I know LGBTQ folks and others who have been "loved" by Christians and churches in that way.

They've been loved right out of church.

The church experience of folks who are perceived as different should not be described by the title of the rock group Nazareth's biggest hit:

"Love Hurts.[iv]"

Love shouldn't be wielded as a weapon to exclude and hurt and shame.

That ain't love.

---

iii. "Love Stinks" (1980) was the J. Geils Band's third biggest hit after "Centerfold" (1982), and "Freeze Frame" (1981). It has been used in several movie soundtracks (including "The Wedding Singer" where it was performed by Adam Sandler). "Love Stinks" was also part of the Soundtrack of My Life that played in my head through most of the '80s ("Love Stinks! Yeah, Yeah!").

iv. Here's something I didn't know until I was fact-checking this book: "Love Hurts" was originally recorded by The Everly Brothers way back in 1960. The hit version I'm familiar with by Nazareth climbed the charts in 1975.

9

Red and Yellow,
Black and White

Growing up, the churches I experienced not only normalized the dominant culture's attitudes and biases, they also embraced white middle-class conservative politics.

My father's politics.

The American flag sat right up front in church with the cross.

We pledged allegiance to the flag, not the cross.

Church differed little from a Fourth of July parade in its glorification of the American way, including American war.

The churches I knew were gung-ho about war and violence as long as they were for the right (i.e. American) reasons.

"Onward Christian Soldiers" cheered on the carpet-bombing, napalming, and grinding up not just of the "enemy" but of our own poorest, disproportionately non-white young men in the Vietnam War.

I never heard a pastor mention the injustice of that conflict.

Or the injustice of racism or segregation or poverty, for that matter.

The only people of color who got mentioned were "the starving children in Africa;" the same ones who were supposed to motivate me to choke down my peas at home.

All that just did not seem right on a very fundamental level.

I recognized my church's intentional injustice blind spots even in late elementary school. I had a heightened, self-sure sense of right and wrong combined with a precocious interest and awareness of current events and history. As you might imagine, this did not enhance my popularity with adults or peers.

As I grew older, I developed a political consciousness of my own. I am sure my leftward drift began as a rebellious reaction to my father's right-wing republicanism. As I internalized progressive viewpoints, my political opinions became one more catalyst for alienation from the churches of my youth.

In those churches, I learned that Jesus was a white middle-class republican afflicted with the same parochialism as the suburban conformists who inhabited the pews.

That was the last kind of person I wanted to worship.

That was the last kind of person I wanted to follow.

That was the last kind of person I wanted to be.

Those who dared to challenge the party line were barely tolerated.

Like Mrs. Thacker.

Mrs. Thacker was my fifth grade Sunday School teacher. Although she was an older, gray-haired woman, she was a Radical, at least for the seventies suburbs I inhabited.

It was 1972, the year Nixon trounced McGovern. I accompanied my dad to the polling place at my school that Election Day. On the way in, someone handed me a postcard of Richard Nixon and his family having a laugh around the piano.

What a great family!

What a great man!

Who could ever even consider voting for someone else?

Mrs. Thacker could.

If you listened, you could hear the murmuring around the church. "Did you hear about Mrs. Thacker? She voted for . . . McGovern." They uttered his name like some folks whisper "cancer," as if speaking its name might invoke its presence.

"Noooo!"

That was nothing, though, compared to the song Mrs. Thacker wanted our class to sing in church.

"Everything Is Beautiful" is a song with a good heart, but treacly execution. Listening to it today it's hard to believe Ray Stevens'[i] harm-

---

i. Ray Stevens had two number one singles in the 70's – "Everything is Beautiful" in 1970 and "The Streak," a novelty hit in 1974. Some of his other big songs were "Ahab the Arab" and "Gitarzan."

less evocation of brotherhood could ever be controversial. Those of us in the fifth grade Sunday School class liked it, and we worked hard on it. It became our song, especially the part about Jesus loving the children.

Us!

I was a big fan . . . there were no r's to rrrroll!

But there's that stuff in the lyrics about not judging people for the length of their hair or the clothes that they wear. Obviously that's about hippies.

Definitely not church folks.

The most troubling thing about the song was which children it said Jesus loved: "Red and yellow, black and white" ones.[ii]

Remember, this was a place and time where mixing the races was just not done. The rainbow of children in the song was iffy. A bunch of church children singing it, conducted (brainwashed) by a Mc-Governite – which was the next thing to being a Communist – was downright subversive.

Jesus loving all the little children was okay.

He just loved them separately.

Red.

And Yellow.

Black.

And white.

Just like in our neighborhoods and our schools . . .

And our churches.

This is why I'm not even sure I remember Mrs. Thacker's name correctly but I am sure she is someone who has inspired me both before and after I returned to church:

We ended up singing "Everything Is Beautiful," just as Mrs. Thacker had planned. . .

In a worship service.

You go, Mrs. Thacker! (Or whatever your name is.)

––––

Mrs. Thacker was a seed planter. The Apostle Paul (remember him)

ii. Although the song was radical (for some) in its time, it has not aged well with its problematic use of colors to define ethnicities.

wrote[iii] that some Christians who share their faith are seed planters and some are harvesters.[iv] The seed planters may never see the harvest. The kernels Mrs. Thacker sowed in fifth grade would be buried deep by layer after layer of my life. They would lay dormant as my faith withered and died, strangled in part by the same narrow-minded attitudes that opposed Mrs. Thacker's effort to teach us that Jesus loved all the little children.

Together.

I would forget and ignore the Mrs. Thackers in the church as I dug into my unChristian position.

Too many Christians I knew confirmed my opinion that churches were filled with judgmental souls afraid of ideas or people that might challenge their docile conventionality. They used their religion to tear apart, not gather together. Conformity preserved their cocoon of self-satisfied stasis.

Twenty years later, when the door of possibility began to open in my heart and (even more important to me) in my mind, those quiet seeds germinated. Nourished by hope,[v] they even began to grow.

Maybe I can be a Christian . . . if I can be one like Mrs. Thacker.

She was a brave non-conformist in the name of Christ, who, I would realize much later, was killed for non-conformity with the prevailing cultural and political attitudes of his time. In her non-conformity, Mrs. Thacker embodied Christ.

That's the kind of Christian I want to be.

That's the kind of person I want to be.

---

iii. In addition to his starring role in the book of Acts that details his conversion and subsequent evangelism, Paul wrote letters (called "Epistles" by Bible folks) that became up to thirteen books in the New Testament. Scholars debate how many of them were actually written by Paul, but it is almost certain that more books in the Bible were written by him than anyone else.

iv. I Corinthians 3:7; also Jesus in John 4:37

v. Skeptics will read that phrase and think, "He means fertilized by the bullshit of religion." That's what I would've thought, too.

10

Santa Claus God

God confused me. Church added to my puzzlement.

When I was in sixth grade I started participating in Youth Group at Lakeside.

Once a month we did something fun – roller skating, bowling, the movies – but there never seemed much connection between the stuff we did and anything spiritual. Except the one time we met at the church for pizza and the youth group leaders brought out a Ouija Board.

It was February and there was snow in the forecast the next day. We asked the Board over and over again if we would get a snow day.

It kept saying, "YES."

It was right!

But were we right to be consulting a Ouija Board? Was God answering our questions by moving the little marker[i] amongst the letters?

Or something else?

Or just us playing a game?

————

By that time I was already asking lots of questions about God.

Sometimes, it seemed God was a lot like Santa Claus. God would give you good stuff IF you were good enough.

That was what Christmas was all about, right?

Christmas was a big deal in my family.

———————

i. It's called a planchette.

Around Thanksgiving, my dad hauled boxes and boxes of decorations down from our attic. We spent the next couple weeks getting the house ready.

By early December, red, green, silver and gold tchotchkes crowded into every corner and covered every surface. Nat King Cole,[ii] Julie Andrews, Bing Crosby, Percy Faith and His Orchestra – and other musicians featured on *Sounds of the Season* gas station giveaway record albums - constantly played on the stereo in the living room. The smells of evergreen and baking Christmas cookies wafted through the house.

My mom loved Christmas, but her stress rose in inverse proportion to the days left to ship packages and mail Christmas cards. After the shopping was done, there was wrapping, signing and addressing that took up time and space at the kitchen table or on TV trays during the annual viewing of *Rudolph the Red Nose Reindeer*.

Excitement and anticipation was tempered by anxiety and overload.

For us kids, the pressure came from knowing we needed to be good . . . or else.

Each year after Thanksgiving a homemade calendar would appear in my room. At each bedtime until Christmas Eve, my mom would stick a star on the day's square.

I'd get a gold star if I'd been unfailingly obedient.

A silver star meant I'd been pretty good.

Green meant I was in the danger zone.

A red star warned I might find coal in my stocking and switches under the tree.

Santa was going to check my calendar when he visited on Christmas Eve.

If there weren't enough gold stars and too many red stars, then all the time I'd spent going through the Sears Christmas Wish Book Catalogue, carefully recording the page numbers and item letters (so the elves and/or my parents would know exactly what I wanted when they read my list) would be for naught.

---

ii. For a few early years I thought Mr. Cole to be chronically tardy. When I asked my mom who was singing, she answered, "That's the late Nat King Cole." On one of his Christmas albums was a song called, "The Little Boy that Santa Claus Forgot" which probably laid an early foundation for my bleeding heart. How could it not? "He's the little boy that Santa Claus forgot, and goodness knows he didn't want a lot. . . I'm so sorry for that laddie, he hasn't got a daddy. . ."

Somehow I always managed to pull it off.

The message I got about Christmas – about God, since it was God's son's birthday – was it was all about me. How Santa treated me – how God treated me – depended on my behavior.

One thing Karen (my wife, we'll bring her into the story later) taught me about Christmas was never to threaten our children with not getting presents because of what they did or didn't do.

"Christmas is about grace," she would say, "God's undeserved gift to the world." So there were no handmade behavior calendars in my kids' rooms when they were little.

(Although it might have been nice to institute them when they became teenagers.)

As a parent, I know how tempting it is to make God just another arrow in the quiver of disciplinary options. If reasoning and threats and time outs don't work, maybe telling a child how pissed off God will be at them can get them to do what you want.

But what does that child learn about God?

What do they learn about our relationship with God?

Growing up I got the impression God's love for me was contingent upon my performance.

Christianity was about what God could do for me if I behaved.

But God's greatest desire is not that we behave, but that we know we are loved.

It is knowing we are loved that frees us to "behave."

Like many churches, mine includes a Children's Sermon during our worship together. Children are invited up to have their special time with the pastor (me!). Often I've heard pastors (mis)use that time for moralizing.

God wants you to share.

God wants you to tell the truth.

God wants you to go to church.

God wants you to be a good citizen.

God wants you to obey your mother and father. (I'm sure moms and dads love that!)

Does God want young people to do all that stuff? Sure!

But we have to be careful to make sure they know obedience is a response to God's love, not the catalyst for it.

I don't always get it right, but this is the question I ask each week when I plan a Children's Sermon:

"How can I tell these young people God loves them no matter what?"

"How can I tell all these people God loves them no matter what?"

There is nothing more important they can know.

In fact, that question permeates the best "regular" sermons as well.

"How can I tell them God loves them no matter what?"

———

It was "No matter what" that was missing from the Christianity I grew up with.

You got what you deserved in life.

You got what you deserved from God.

Sure, we sang "Jesus Loves Me," but Christianity's conditional contract had not-so-fine print that read,

"Jesus loves me IF . . ."

Jesus loves me IF I listen to my mom and dad. Jesus loves me IF I get good grades and don't get into trouble at school. Jesus loves me IF I do my best in Little League and Scouts and IF I get enough gold stars on my calendar.

As I look back at the religion into which I was indoctrinated growing up, it is grace that was absent – or at least kept under wraps in case someone might get the wrong idea. If they thought God loves them no matter what, who knows what they'd do!

But that's the most right idea of all!

Once someone realizes God loves them no matter what, the thing they might do is love that way in return.

11

Camp Hanover

I appreciate the comforts of modernity as much as anyone, but they shield us from the wonders of creation. Young people in particular need respite from manufactured reality. We all need room for organic awe and wonder.

During my unChristian twenties I worked for two years as a counselor at a secular Wilderness Camp for delinquent youth. The young men who spent a year or more in our intensive program built the platform tents they lived in, planned and took weeks-long backpack and canoe trips, and chopped lots of firewood to get through the winters in the North Carolina mountains.

The camp – and others like it – had the lowest recidivism rate of any residential program in the state. That achievement was attributable not just to the structure of the program but especially to the nature (pun intended) of the backwoods environment in which the program took place.

Unmediated interaction with creation can change people.

––––

Prior to my wilderness camp employment, my only experience with overnight camp was Camp Hanover, a Presbyterian Camp in Virginia.

Camp Hanover was nothing like the camp for troubled youth.

Except this . . .

It was transformative.

Most of the transformation was not effective anytime that would be considered "soon."

I have written about people who were seed planters.

Camp Hanover was a seed-planting place.

I spent one week at Camp Hanover in each of the summers after my fourth, fifth, and sixth grade school years. As I retrace my journey to the follower of Christ I am today, I realize the memories and the influence of those three weeks are greatly disproportionate to actual time spent at Camp Hanover.

The second year my group had a counselor from England which was pretty cool in itself. On the first day he told us that later in the week we would be taking a "night-hike with torches!"

Torches!

The anticipation built as we pictured walking through the dark woods, our way illuminated only by the fiery sticks we held aloft.

Imagine our disappointment when we found out "torch" was only British for "flashlight."

The night-hike was pretty cool, though.

The English Counselor looms large in my Camp Hanover memories for another word, one that is the same in the United States as it is in Britain.

"Damn."

At chapel each night, a different group presented a skit. They were pretty standard moralistic tripe. He was determined ours would be different.

Our counselor guided us to construct a scenario in which a new kid entered our school. A Jewish kid. He was initially rejected by everyone, and ultimately betrayed in a cruel prank.[i] One of the kids who participated in the prank felt guilty, and tried to make it up to him by inviting him to his house for a party.

The last line was the Jewish kid saying, "I don't want to come to your damn party!"

It was shocking! Cursing at all was unacceptable. This was in chapel!

I wonder if my counselor got into trouble for that. I hope not.

It impacted me – I still remember it, not the exact plot but the point

---

i. I am sorry that for the life of me I can't remember the details of the prank, and would feel disloyal to my counselor, who must be in a retirement home in England by now, if I made something up.

(and the word) over 40 years later! Like Mrs. Thacker, my English counselor gave me a glimpse of a kind of Christianity that departed from the flaccid monochrome conformity of my childhood churches.

Those glimpses didn't keep me from deserting the church for a time, but they helped mold the form of faith I grew into – or more accurately, grew in me – when I came back.

At camp I was loved unconditionally by cool young adults, even though I was a pain in the ass sometimes and even when they had to walk me all the way across the camp to the nurse's office in the middle of the night because my IBS flared up.

The loving presence of God was expressed in the compassionate care of counselors and other camp staff. The counselors in particular embodied empathy and grace as they wiped away tears, assuaged fears, built group cohesion, negotiated peace between temporary enemies, and responded to the ongoing and often inconvenient needs of young people away from home, many for the first time.

Camp Hanover was not an institution of indoctrination like you may have seen in the documentary film *Jesus Camp*.[ii] God was not forced down my throat but rather acknowledged and honored as an abiding, unconditionally loving presence in the lives of campers and counselors.

Participation and even questions were not only allowed but encouraged during Bible Studies and worship.

As I look back, I wonder how much of my own style of ministry was influenced by those weeks at Camp Hanover.

All of this serious stuff is not to negate perhaps THE essential ingredient of the camp experience.

FUN!

If it wasn't fun then no one would show up for the other stuff.

We often make the mistake of divorcing fun from Christianity.

Growing up, religion was a dour affair. So many rules! Don't run in church, don't talk in church, don't dress too comfortable for church,

---

ii. *Jesus Camp* is a 2006 documentary about a right-wing Christian camp whose leaders believe their mission is to train kids to be part of an "army of God" to foist their narrow-mindedness on America. It's scary stuff, but it does have its memorably ironic moments like Ted Haggard preaching a sermon against homosexuality. (You may remember he was later caught in a sexual liaison with another man. The ones who condemn the loudest may have something to hide.)

take your hat off in church, sit up straight and pay attention in church. If that's religion, then it is a wonder any young person sticks with it once they have a choice.

Any real fun was confined to Youth Ministry and not allowed to seep out into "real" worship or to infect any adults not engaged with young people.

But Jesus undoubtedly knew how to have fun. He was fully human, not just the solemn parts. His first miracle was at a wedding;[iii] turning water into wine sure sounds like a catalyst for fun! He was the kind of person you invited to your party. People liked to be around him.

What I experienced at Camp Hanover was that following Jesus could be fun, at least sometimes. Along with s'mores and homemade blueberry ice cream, I had a taste of the JOY that is at the heart of our relationship with God.

And, at Camp Hanover, I first heard of C. S. Lewis.

iii. John 2:1-11

12

Undragoning

C. S. Lewis wrote the book that would become the most influential for me (except the Bible) in my return to faith. That book, *Mere Christianity*, is written for adults.

Lewis also wrote a series of seven books for children, *The Chronicles of Narnia*. Narnia is a fantastic realm where animals speak and the battle between good and evil is played out in stories inspired by ancient myths and medieval fairy tales. Like all the best children's books, the lessons and stories of the Narnia books defy age. Rereading them as an adult, I experienced the wonder of a child while processing the allegories through the wisdom of experience.

During quiet time each afternoon during my last year at Camp Hanover, a female counselor read aloud from the third Narnia book, *The Voyage of the Dawn Treader.*[i] It begins like this:

"There was a boy named Eustace Clarence Scrubb, and he almost deserved it."

Eustace Scrubb is an unlikeable boy who enters Narnia through an enchanted painting.[ii] He ends up on a ship called the Dawn Treader, where he complains constantly, going on about how much smarter he is than everyone else. He is also quite lazy.

Once, when the ship docked at an island and everyone had work to

---

i. It was the third published, but in some lists *The Voyage of the Dawn Treader* is listed as fifth because that is chronologically when the events of the book take place.

ii. English children are transported to Narnia through various means in the series, most famously by way of a magical wardrobe.

do, Eustace snuck away. He hid in a cave and blundered upon a great dragon treasure. Being Eustace, he imagined how being rich would give him the opportunity to get even with everyone who had ever slighted him.

He thought, "greedy, dragonish thoughts."

Eustace played in the treasure and put on a gold bracelet. Then he fell asleep.

When he awoke, he had been transformed into a dragon. His dragon-arm throbbed with pain. The gold bracelet was now too small. When he returned to the ship, the others attacked him until they realized who he was.

Being a dragon helped Eustace see what a scoundrel he had been. Although people were initially repulsed by his dragon-ness, he did what he could to be helpful. He tried to change.

But he could not stop being a dragon.

When it was time for the ship to sail, Eustace could not fit. He would have to be left behind on the island, alone.

Eustace cried big, dragon-tears.

One day the great lion Aslan arrived. If you've read the Narnia books, you know Aslan is the Christ figure. He is powerful, but also merciful and compassionate. In one of the books, he dies a sacrificial death. (But that's not the end of the story!)

In this book Aslan takes Eustace to a garden where there is clear, cool water. Eustace knows the water will make his arm feel better. Aslan tells him he can get into the water, but he'll have to get undressed first.

He remembers dragons have skin like snakes that can be shed. So Eustace starts tugging away at his dragon skin. But under each layer there is another. Three times he peels his skin away, each time becoming more and more desperate and despairing.

He fears he will have to remain a dragon forever.

He fears he will have to remain alone forever.

Then Aslan says, "You will have to let me undress you."

Even fear of Aslan's claws isn't enough to stop Eustace from lying on his back and asking the lion to tear off his dragon skin.

Here is Lewis' description of what happens next, from Eustace's perspective:

The very first tear he made was so deep I thought it had gone right through into my heart. And when he began pulling the skin off, it hurt worse than anything I've ever felt. The only thing that made me able to bear it was just the pleasure of peeling the stuff off . . .

And there I was as smooth and soft as a peeled switch and smaller than I had been. Then he caught hold of me – I didn't like that much for I was very tender underneath now that I'd no skin on – and threw me into the water. It smarted like anything but only for a moment. After that it became perfectly delicious and as soon as I started swimming and splashing I found that all the pain had gone from my arm. And then I saw why. I had turned into a boy again . . .

After a bit the lion took me out and dressed me . . . in new clothes.

I remember how it felt to be twelve, sweating on my cot on a sweltering summer afternoon, listening to my counselor read about the undragoning of Eustace.

It cut me to the heart.

I saw myself in Eustace. I complained. I was often lazy.

I assumed I was smarter than everyone else.

I had "dragonish, greedy thoughts."

Eustace recognized he had messed up. He recognized he was messed up.

Most important, he realized he could not help himself. He realized only Aslan could change him. Only Aslan could save him.

I don't know if I made the Aslan-Christ connection then, but it planted a seed of the experience of grace.

Someday, like Eustace, I would realize that I could not help myself.

———

When you walk into a bookstore, you can browse for hours in the self-help section. Those books tell you how you can get your life together and improve yourself and be happier.

There are lots of self-help books.

The Bible ain't one of them.

The Bible is a You-Can't-Help-Yourself Book.

Christianity is a You-Can't-Help-Yourself faith.

Becoming a follower of Jesus is not about trying hard.

You become a follower of Jesus when you stop trying because you realize Jesus has done everything you need already.

That realization is faith.

Faith is not something you do, or strive for, or achieve.

Faith happens when you stop trying to do, or to strive, or to achieve.

Faith happens when you realize that when Jesus said, "It is finished" on the cross, he really meant it.

––––––

We didn't have time to finish *The Voyage of the Dawn Treader* in a week of camp quiet times. On the last day I asked the female counselor who had been reading to write down the name of the book for me. I still remember the feel of the scratchy strokes on the back of my hand as she wrote "Voyage of the Dawn Treader" there with a pen.

When I got home, I checked out the book from the Richmond Public Library and finished it in a few greedy gulps.

I went on to read the other six Narnia books, but soon found out I would have to finish the series in Florida.

Florida

13

The Sunshine State

The summer after sixth grade a metaphorical nuclear bomb dropped into the life of the Happy Little Simpsons. One evening after supper[i] my dad announced we were moving to Florida. Seaboard Coast Line Railroad had transferred him to Jacksonville, and there was no choice.

A month later, the Simpsons left Woodman Terrace. I was about to become the New Kid.

It is difficult for me to look at pictures of myself from the first year in Florida.

In elementary school, I had been the last chosen for sports teams at recess. I wore "Husky" pants and my nickname was "The Good Simp Blimp."

Seventh grade me looks a little less "husky," but not like anyone who would have been known for anything but a brain, if that. My hair encases my head like a black helmet; the effect is reminiscent of the top of a cartoon ant's head. I've got straight-across bangs, which continued around the side of my head about halfway over my ears. Ridiculously large, undoubtedly uncool, never in style, black-plastic framed glasses dominate my doughy face. That is if you can see my face; you may be blinded by the brilliant sparkle of all the metal in my mouth.

"Awkward" would be a generous description of the seventh grade

---

i. In the south "supper" is the evening meal and "dinner" is a big meal in the middle of the day, usually on Sunday.

David Simpson.[ii]

Looking at those pictures from my earliest adolescence when I was the New Kid in Town, I'm amazed I made any friends.

It took a while.

After attending neighborhood schools in Virginia, my new Seventh Grade Center in Jacksonville required a twice-daily forty-five minute ride over the St. Johns River and into the inner city.

When a Federal Judge ordered Jacksonville schools to integrate a few years before we arrived, a plan was hatched to mitigate the white uproar. Inner city (African-American) students were bused out to white neighborhoods for all of elementary school and disproportionately displaced for middle and high school. Suburban (white) kids would only be bused into the city center for two years. Some downtown schools were rechristened Sixth Grade and Seventh Grade Centers where theoretically all the students – red and yellow, black and white – would spend two years in an urban melting pot.

But that wasn't exactly what happened. Lots of white families bailed on the integrated school system entirely. Private schools flourished. Parents who couldn't afford all twelve years of refuge at least got their kids out for those sixth and seventh grade years at "n----- schools."

Guess what kind of institutions established and ran many of the white sanctuary schools.

Churches.

I didn't think too deeply about that until I got older and became more attuned to the racial history of My People – southern white folks.

It was just another demonstration of the church's complicity in maintaining the separate but (not really) equal status quo.

Which in turn is another reason for me not to want anything to do with the God on whose behalf the church spoke and acted.

What churches choose to do matters. Plans and decisions may make sense because they are popular and, as in the case of the separatist schools, financially lucrative. But the church is the tangible manifestation of Jesus in the world – the very Body of Christ.

When churches act and advocate to maintain an unjust status quo,

---

ii. I did not become "Dave" until the wilderness camp job I mentioned earlier. Counselors were addressed by the campers as "Chief Your Name Here." Chief David just seemed too long somehow, so I became Chief Dave, and forever Dave.

members and outsiders alike conflate the attitudes and actions of the church with the nature of God. It is no wonder that for many – not just in the south but all over this country, and not just in the past but to this very day – God is a white man who believes in keeping the races separate like the church schools did in Jacksonville.

———

The n-word[iii] was thrown around with abandon in that place and time. If someone made a mistake, they were told they "could mess up a one car n----- funeral." White culture was infected with the casual racism of unchallenged prejudice.

One of my friends occasionally wore to school a T-shirt signed by Lester Maddox, the former governor of Georgia famous for wielding an axe handle while chasing black customers out of the restaurant he owned. The shirt featured a picture of Maddox and of course an axe handle. No one – teacher or student – ever remarked upon the shirt to my knowledge. It was literally unremarkable.[iv]

I could defensively assert that I owned no racist apparel, nor did I ever utter the n-word. But neither did I ever challenge or even question those who did.

Silence connotes assent.

Silence in the face of oppression and injustice makes one complicit.

My silence, especially as I came to be sensitive to matters of race, is an embarrassment and a sin that has been repeated too many times in my life, and not just as a child.

It was a sin I never heard identified in any of the churches my family attended.

Let's not give my family a pass, either.

Although there were no explicit racist statements and I never heard my parents use the n-word, there was implicit acceptance of "the way things are."

Traumatized by the change in my school situation, I panicked when

———

iii. I struggled with the decision to include the n-word in this book more than I did any of the other profanities I have chosen to employ. That is the way racists talked – and still talk. I decided not to repeat their hatred-fueled vulgarity.

iv. Two more Lester Maddox factoids: He was governor of Georgia when Martin Luther King Jr. died in 1968 and denied a request that King's body lie in state in the Georgia capital; and he is immortalized in Randy Newman's song appropriately titled, "Rednecks." I would add that he justified his racism with the Bible but that's obvious, right?

my mom and dad told me we were going to try a new church, bigger than the one in the neighborhood we initially attended. On the way to the Big Church, I blurted out, "I don't want to go to a black church!" I'm not sure why I thought it might be a "black church" other than my experience in Jacksonville schools. Probably, I'd just had enough change.

My mom responded, "There won't be any black people, I'm sure."

This was meant to be reassuring. It was.

But it was not part of her cultural DNA to say something instead like, "If it turns out to be a black church that wouldn't be a bad thing."

I grew up listening to stories about contented slaves and fighting The Lost Cause[v] from my great grandfather, who heard them from his grandfather. Many southern families are steeped in that rotten legacy, perfumed by the idealized and idolatrous retelling through the generations. It is difficult to understand for those who did not grow up with it.

That sense of family heritage and honor makes it personal when people these days start talking about tearing down statues of Robert E. Lee and other (literal) Losers.

In Richmond, where I spent those first twelve years, the ritziest homes in town, owned by those of top social rank, lined Monument Avenue. The street was designed with a grassy median where statues of Lee and his Confederate comrades J.E.B. Stuart and Stonewall Jackson could look down from their horses toward downtown, where the folks of color lived who needed to be reminded of their place lest they get too 'uppity.'

Lee, Stuart and Jackson[vi] were venerated in elementary school history class. My family took trips to Civil War battlefields. Stuart was killed not too far from my Richmond house. We made occasional pilgrimages to the site. My mom especially saw things from the south side of the trenches; *Gone with the Wind* was not just her favorite movie; it was

---

v. It is said that history is written by the winners, but The Lost Cause is a reinterpretation of history from the supposed noble perspective of the Confederacy, complete with bittersweet sepia-toned nostalgia and hagiographies of southern generals.

vi. Lee's loyalty to Virginia (over his country, as if that were a good thing), Stuart's bravery as a scout ("The eyes of the Confederate army"), and Jackson's resilience like a Stone Wall were ideals for which good southern boys like me were encouraged to strive.

a picture of the South she had been taught to believe by her people.

I bought some of that then. In ninth grade we were asked to write a paper about our hero, and I wrote about that great, great, great, etc. grandfather. I retold the daring exploits of his capture by the Yankees when he tried to retake some of the horses they had stolen from the Grays. After being sentenced to death, he outwitted those damn Yankees by cutting a hole in the back of a tent and escaping.

I proudly and cluelessly turned in the masterpiece to my African-American teacher.

I had never been taught empathy for those whose experience was different than that of my people.

You might think my parents would have put me in one of those academies for seventh grade to rescue me from the inner city, integrated experience. But we were strictly a public school family. That was certainly not due to any progressive racial attitudes held by my parents. My dad simply wasn't going to pay for something he could darn well get for free.

So I rode the cheese wagon each day to Matthew W. Gilbert Seventh Grade Center. It was a scary new world.

Most of my classes turned out to be segregated. The advanced courses were almost exclusively white; kids of color weren't believed to be able to succeed.

Or it was feared they might.

I was most aware of my new school environment during the several-block walk to the field on which we played during PE. Our instructors herded us past rundown row homes, boarded up shacks, and vacant lots strewn with trash. Our field of sand and weeds was not much better. The smell of coffee from the nearby Maxwell House plant infused the neighborhood with a bitter background bouquet.

———

During the first few weeks that fall, I was the New Kid without any friends. I lacked friend-making skills like talking to someone I didn't know. Although I still proudly identify as an introvert,[vii] back then I

---

vii. INFP (Introvert iNtuitive Feeling Perceiver) for you Myers-Briggs folks keeping score at home. I used to be an INTP (Thinker instead of Feeler). Those of you not familiar with the Myers-Briggs personality inventory, Google is your friend (says the Thinker). I'm so sorry (says the Feeler).

was just painfully shy.

I experienced my alienation most acutely on the trips to school and back. I stood alone and apart from the other kids at the bus stop. They all seemed to know each other. Every morning was like standing outside a party to which I hadn't been invited.

On the bus, I was an island in a sea of rowdy camaraderie.

The first kids to notice me were the bullies. Like hyenas, bullies pick off those who are separated from the herd. I had no defense other than hoping my inadequacies would not be worth the trouble of torment or even notice.

It wasn't long before I got some ridicule; nothing as creative as "The Good Simp Blimp," though. The tired taunting was more on the level of "Four Eyes" and "Metal Mouth."

My mantra was, "Ignore them and they'll find somebody else to pick on."

I pretended I couldn't hear them, and found the scenery we passed twice a day much more interesting than it was. I clutched my *Star Trek* lunchbox[viii] closer, like a metal teddy bear.

Yes, it is a wonder I survived. I was red meat for any bully. Glasses, braces, pudgy, no friends, no desire or ability to fight, *Star Trek* . . .

Let's make this an uplifting message for any young people reading this who feel similarly uncool. It does get better. You're not alone. The improvement may not happen in school like it eventually did for me, but eventually you'll find a group where you fit in. Your school or neighborhood (or church) is like a terrarium – an enclosed environment with mostly homogenous species. But once you break out of that jar you'll find the wider world is much more varied including (surprise!) people like you.

Someday you may win hundreds of thousands of dollars on game shows.

"I'll take 'Where are those bullies now for 200, Alex!'"

For now, don't let the bullies get you down.

After a while, I made friends who were also in advanced classes and who talked about *Star Trek* and acted out scenes from *SWAT* (a violent police show I had to beg my parents to let me watch) and tried to

---

viii. But you'd already guessed I had one of those, right?

hypnotize each other using instructions we found in a book.

We were never meant to go through life alone. I believe now that God created us for relationship with God and with each other. Friends are therefore both a confirmation and a manifestation of our very nature.

God very definitely shows up in the people who we love and who love us.

Even when (like me for a very long time) we don't realize it.

14

A Pronounced Disagreement

During my year at Matthew W. Gilbert Seventh Grade Center, I encountered a teacher who used the classroom to proselytize his religious point of view.

It's not what you think.

———

One class period each day at the Seventh Grade Center was taken up with something called the "Pre-Vocational Wheel." You got to rotate quickly through a series of potential careers; quickly was good in case you sucked at one of them like I did in Woodshop. The birdhouse I made would have been condemned by any reasonable avian housing inspector, and tested my parents' commitment to always find something good to say about my efforts.

Another spoke in the Pre-Vocational Wheel was Business Administration.

All I remember content-wise was a bunch of filing practice along with a smattering of business letter writing. As long as you were handy with the alphabet and could spell "Sincerely," you could ace Business Administration.

The B.A. teacher was a guy who managed to be both laid back and arrogant at the same time. He was arrogant about his casualness. You probably know the type: anti-establishment rebels in their youth who sold out but have convinced themselves it was on their terms.

This is why I'll call him Mr. Smythe:

While reviewing one of the scintillating filing exercises, Mr. Smythe corrected me about the pronunciation of "Smythe." I said it like "Smith" and he said it should be "Smithy." I would not let the matter rest, although I admit I was unsure and arguing mainly out of boredom.

I've just spent a half hour on Google reading phonetic expressions of "Smythe" on various websites, as well as listening to MP3s where they are available. None of them has "Smithy" as a possible pronunciation.

File that under "L for Loser," Mr. Smythe!

And now, at least in this book, you are "Mr. Smythe."

Yes, it is a little pathetic that I am still fighting this battle over forty years later. I'm including this in part to demonstrate a critical facet of my personality.

I don't like to be wrong.

That trait was reinforced by everyone telling me how smart I am from the time I can remember . . . with the occasional exception of dolts like Mr. Smythe.

My need to be right inhibited me from even considering returning to church as an adult. It would mean admitting I was wrong to leave in the first place.

Knowing the right answers was (and still is) a big part of my identity and Mr. Smythe offended that by correcting me unjustly. Like stereotypical middle schoolers and college sophomores, I had an overdeveloped belief in my ability to adjudicate justice and truth . . . especially when I was the self-perceived injured party.

It took (is taking) a while to grow out of that, too.

It's a process.

The second thing I remember about Mr. Smythe is the day he decided to evangelize. He wanted all of us seventh graders to see the light, or more exactly, his light. That meant sharing his view of God and casting off our various religious indoctrinations.

Some of you more conservative Christian folks are metaphorically on your feet applauding. "Hear! Hear! Religious freedom! God back in the schools!"

But not so fast . . .

I don't remember what precipitated the conversation. Maybe we were filing something under Jesus (I imagine Mr. Smythe pronouncing it Gee-SEUSS, but I know I'm making that up). Perhaps we were learning how to address a cardinal or a bishop in a business letter.

Something got him going.

"I know most of you go to church. Your parents probably make you."

He paused.

"What a waste of time!"

In spite of my baseline of antipathy toward Mr. Smythe, he was verbalizing some of my unspoken angst. He had my attention.

"I'm an atheist."

Mr. Smythe was the first person I ever heard say they did not believe in God.

"There is no God. And most people know that. They just don't want to admit it."

Whoa! No God!

I didn't like church but I had never gone that far. I hadn't allowed myself to venture there in seventh grade. I didn't even know it was an option.

"Your parents, they don't believe any of it either but they go to church and jump through all the hoops and go through the motions for the same reason all of you do stupid things: peer pressure. The same reason they buy big houses and expensive cars: peer pressure. Keeping up with the Joneses.

"The difference between your parents and me is they don't have the guts to say it: God does not exist."

Now wait a minute. That wasn't true. About my parents. He didn't even know my mom or dad.

My hand shot up.

He was anticipating, hoping for, an objection. "Yes, David?"

"My father was church treasurer and he sings in the choir. My mom taught Vacation Bible School. We pray before every meal at home and at bedtime. My parents definitely believe in God."

Mr. Smythe shook his head. I didn't know yet what condescending meant but that's what he was. "David, what does your father do for a living?"

"He's an accountant," I said proudly.

"Well, that explains it," Mr. Smythe proclaimed, his voice ringing with the triumph of besting a twelve year old. "I'm sure most of his business comes from people in the church. The church is all about money for him . . . business contacts. If he didn't go to church, he wouldn't have clients."

With that, he turned to the next item of what he was supposed to be teaching us about The Wonderful World of Filing. I didn't get a chance to respond.

It wouldn't have mattered. I'm sure if I had told him my dad wasn't that kind of accountant – that he didn't need clients because he worked for the railroad – Mr. Smythe would just have replied that the expectation to go to church was simply part of the corporate culture. He should know, teaching Business Administration and all.

I was pissed at Mr. Smythe.

I realize writing this I still am.

The memory of his attempted atheistic proselytization undergirds my conviction that teacher-imposed religion has no place in public schools. Some Christians advocate teacher-led prayer in the name of "Getting God back into the schools."[i] But they fail to consider that once you open the door to any religion, all religions – and anti-religion – are going to walk right in.

It would have been no more appropriate for Mr. Smythe to tell us we should be Christians, or Buddhists or Wiccans, than it was for him to promote his atheism in Business Administration class.

On the other hand, maybe Buddhism would have been more appropriate, a sort of Pre-Vocational Dharma Wheel.[ii] But I digress (again).

Religion, or more exactly faith in God (or not), is too important to be entrusted to the whims of a child's class assignment. I venture to say this is true for believers of all sorts as well as non-believers. In a pluralistic society, it is just as wrong for my child to be encouraged to pray five times a day facing Mecca by a Muslim teacher as it is for a Christian teacher to strong-arm a Muslim child to participate in prayers in the name of Jesus, or for a child from an atheist family to be pressured

---

i. As if God could ever be forcibly absented from anywhere. By the way, the implied ability of humans to expel God from school or any other space does not enhance the argument that God is omnipresent and omnipotent.

ii. The Dharma Wheel is a symbol associated with Buddhism and other related religions such as Hinduism. It looks sort of like the wheel on an old sailing ship.

to be part of any prayer at all.

And it would be blasphemous – I do not use that term lightly – to attempt crafting a milquetoast address to a generic deity (who may or may not exist) so as to please everyone.

Prayer should be allowed in public schools. . . and it is. The old saying is true: "As long as there are math tests, there will be prayer in school." Students should be allowed to pray individually or in groups in which they voluntarily lead and participate free from the actual or implicit coercion of authority.

I do not hold Mr. Smythe responsible in any way for my eventual conversion to his unspiritual "side." My offense at his screed was more about my parents' faith, or lack thereof, than my own. I don't ever recall doubting the sincerity of Mom or Dad's belief in God or Jesus.

Although I did not acknowledge it at the time, even in seventh grade I was already well down the road in my journey to rejecting God. Mr. Smythe's atheistic altar call did nothing to further my exit from faith. If anything, he made atheism seem as unattractive as Christianity. He was just as judgmental as the aggressive Christians I encountered; both Mr. Smythe and those Christians seemed to be more concerned with being right than they were about me.

15

A Hell of a Chapter

One summer between middle school grades I devoured all twenty-two chapters of Revelation[i] in one night.

I didn't get much sleep that night.

Without any framework to understand the symbolism, there was nothing for me but beasts emerging from the sea, destructive horsemen, plagues and pestilence, and the end of just about everything.

Cool!

For a thirteen year old who would soon discover Stephen King novels it was all pretty awesome. What could be better than being scared by creatures and calamities and combustion? The whole world blew up!

That of course was not the reaction I was "supposed" to have.

The neighbor kid who urged me to read about The End of the World was concerned about my immortal soul; his goal was not to provide me with *The Exorcist*-level entertainment.

Frank lived down the street and was a year or so younger than me. On the night I read Revelation, he walked up to a group of us neighbor boys. He was way overdressed for a Sunday night in the humid Florida summer.

It turned out Frank and his family had been to some kind of revival at their church. They were Southern Baptists like most people in Jacksonville, so they usually went to church twice on Sundays anyway.

---

i. The most mispronounced book in the Bible is the last one. The full name is The Revelation to John, but you'll hear even educated clergy preach about "Revelations."

But tonight was, Frank told us, something special. They had a speaker from out of town who laid out God's end times script featuring The Rapture.

It was the first time I'd ever heard of The Rapture, so I asked Frank what the hell he was talking about.

"The end of the world! It's gonna happen any day now. And those people who are good with God are gonna get taken up to heaven in the blink of an eye. It could happen right now! If I disappear you'll know what happened. Planes are gonna crash because their pilots are gonna get raptured."

At this point my inner nerd kicked in and I made a mental note: "Rapture" was a verb, too.

Frank continued, "All that's gonna be left is their clothes!"

Another guy asked, "You mean the ones who disappear are going to be naked?"

Frank was annoyed at the detour. "I guess."

"Cool." That kid was close to being a convert right there.

Naked girls in heaven.

Cool indeed!

Frank tried to get his sermon back on track. "They'll get robes. White robes, I think." Frank had already mastered the unfortunate Christian tendency, particularly prevalent in preachers and Sunday School teachers, to fill in theological gaps with authoritatively delivered speculation rather than simply admitting, "I don't know."

He continued, fervent in his concern for our souls.

Or for being right.

"Anyway, you don't understand! You don't want to miss out on The Rapture. What happens next on earth is The Tribulation. If you don't get raptured you're gonna go through years of wars and plagues and evil. Then you go to hell where you're gonna burn forever but you won't burn up. So you better get right with God!"

"Uh huh," I replied.

Frank unwound some more of the yarn that'd been spun at the revival. "And at the end of time there's gonna be The Final Judgment. Your whole life will be projected like a movie on the clouds and everybody's gonna see it."

I swear that's what he said. The rest of the conversation is based on the bare bones of what I remember, but I clearly recall Frank telling us our lives were going to be projected on the clouds.

Everything.

In front of everybody.

This was a little concerning as there were things – new and wonderful but private things – I didn't want projected on any screen. But even for a middle school kid like me, it sounded pretty ridiculous. "Where do you get this stuff, Frank?"

"It's in Revelations." Of course Frank added the s.[ii]

We questioned Frank for a while until that got boring and we got to talking about more important and plausible things like UFOs and something one of us heard about a strange sphere of light that came up out of a lake and some kid disappeared.

Then there was some talk about baseball. The conversation drifted like the summer breeze as we discussed other random stuff. Somewhere in there, of course, we might have speculated what sex might be like. Or probably just what girls might be like.

Naked.

If you've been a middle school boy the flow of this conversation will seem natural.

But back to hell. That's what this chapter is about.

Don't worry, we're getting there.

Maybe I should put that another way.

My usual routine that summer was to stay up most of the night tuning in far-away broadcasts on my Radio Shack shortwave radio. I wrote to the stations with reception reports and got colorful cards[iii] back covered in exotic stamps from Europe, South America, and even Africa.

That night, I didn't turn on the radio. I got the black genuine-leather-cover Bible with my name (all three names!) stamped in sparkly gold letters off my bookcase shelf where it had pretty much sat since I got it on my 9th birthday. I laid back on the bed and opened it up. The

---

ii. We all have our equivalents to fingernails on a chalkboard. "Revelations" is up there with misusing "its" and "it's" for me.

iii. Technically QSL cards. I had quite a collection. Some of the stations sent brochures and booklets about their countries. Radio Havana sent a packed packet of propaganda. I'm probably still on some government list for communicating with Cuba in middle school.

print sure was tiny! There were no notes to help me understand what I was reading.

It was not the impenetrable King James Version of which my Southern Baptist friend would have approved. But its Revised Standard Version text, based directly on the KJV, was still a pretty tough read for most adults, even more so a middle schooler.[iv]

I journeyed through those twenty-two apocalyptic chapters. I was riveted the same way I would be when I read '*Salem's Lot*[v] that summer. I found nothing about The Rapture exactly, but the world definitely ended.

There weren't any movies of lives projected on clouds. But there was a lot about judgment.

As darkly cool as Revelation seemed, the judgment stuff did bother me some. Frank's exegesis provided the only interpretive framework I had for all the symbolism. Revelation never came up in sermons at my church, and certainly not in Sunday School.

I don't remember any mention of hell at the churches we attended either. Those safe, suburban congregations focused so much on being "nice" that they would have been uncomfortable considering God not practicing Southern Hospitality.

Hell was for other people, anyway.

I figured I must be okay with God.

But I was worried about Jerry Lewis.

———

I was a faithful watcher of the annual Labor Day Muscular Dystro-

---

iv. "What is the best Bible translation, Pastor Dave?" That's a question I am often asked. Dozens of English language Bibles cram bookstore shelves and Amazon screens. The Bible was originally written in Hebrew (Hebrew Scriptures) and Greek (New Testament). The 1611 King James Version was not the first English Bible, but it dominated the market for hundreds of years. English has changed a great deal since its introduction, but many still love its poetry. That's fine, but what's not fine are "King James Only" Christians who insist all other translations are perversions. That's just silly. The Revised Standard Version (RSV) of my childhood Bible was first introduced in 1901. Some more recent translations I use for study are the New Revised Standard Version (NRSV) and the Common English Bible (CEB). For simply reading the Bible, it's hard to beat the accessibility of Eugene Peterson's "The Message." But ultimately I suggest just going to a bookstore and taking some time to compare what's available. The best Bible translation is the one you will actually read.

v. Stephen King's second published book (after *Carrie*). It's about vampires. David Soul, famous for the 70's TV Show *Starsky and Hutch* (he was Hutch) starred in the film adaptation.

phy Telethon. Jerry stayed up all night and the next day to raise money for "his" kids who had muscular dystrophy. At the end of it all he sang that song about walking in the rain.[vi] He always cried.

He really cared!

Every year I would call "the number at the bottom of your screen" and pledge a dollar. That was my whole weekly allowance, at least when I started pledging in elementary school. My mom thought it was great. She told me I should have a "pet charity," whatever that meant.

My friends and I even talked about putting on a Backyard Carnival for Dystrophy with one of the free kits Jerry was always touting. That got as far as our plans to build a submarine or to construct a stage and put on a play.

Jerry Lewis was a Good Guy.

Somewhere I learned he was Jewish. God gave me a sticky brain and that was one of the random facts that stuck. But when it came to hell, this information caused me some concern. If people without Jesus burn forever without burning up, then Jerry Lewis will burn forever without burning up.

And he's a Good Guy.

I acknowledge any thought process with *The Nutty Professor*[vii] as its lynchpin sounds kind of ridiculous.

But it is basically the same train of thought – without the centrality of Mr. Lewis – that made the idea of hell a repellant rather than an attractant.

Some Christians believe hell is a great motivator for getting folks, especially unChristians, in line. "Get right with God or else" is con-

---

vi. "You'll Never Walk Alone," originally from the Rogers and Hammerstein musical, *Carousel*.

vii. *The Nutty Professor* is considered Lewis' masterpiece of comedy by some critics and many fans. Honestly, I'm not a fan of the 1963 film or its 1995 remake starring Eddie Murphy. In his later interviews and appearances, Lewis revealed a personality more like that of Buddy Love, the professor's obnoxious alter-ego in the films. He apparently is not the paragon Good Guy I thought he was. But then, who is? A foundational belief of Christianity is that we are all messed up – we all have Buddy Love lurking inside. I know I do. And as I've said before one big reason I believe the truth of Christianity is that it so truthfully describes human (my) nature. I embrace the Lutheran flavor of Christianity in part because Martin Luther summarized this nature so aptly – each Christian is fully sinner (messed up) and fully saint (cleaned up). If you want to impress your local Lutheran clergyperson, the theological term for this saint/sinner duality is *Simul justus et peccator*.

sidered mighty fine evangelism.

No matter that evangelism means sharing good news. Such folks lack a sense of irony.

They think if you terrify folks, they'll jump into the water (of baptism) to avoid the fire (of hell).

I don't think they put it in those words exactly, but the concept is common among Christians, and not just of the fire and brimstone variety.

"Do you really want to spend eternity in hell? If not, you need to give your life to Jesus."

But that's like trying to sell umbrellas to folks who don't think it's going to rain.

If you don't believe in God, you probably don't believe in hell. It's like threatening someone with a gun when they know all you've got are your fingers cocked behind your coat.

Threatening theology was a primary reason I left the Christian faith behind.[viii]

Threatening theology was a primary reason I was away so long.

It wasn't just that I couldn't reconcile the idea of a loving, forgiving God eternally torturing people.

Although that did seem awfully excessive. Even petty.

"You won't worship Me?! I'll show you Who's the Boss!"

Was God really that insecure?

What was the point of hell? Punishment should have a purpose, right? Otherwise it is only revenge.

Or sadism.

Shouldn't there be some gain from the pain?

Sure, make people suffer until they admit they're wrong. Then forgive them. But if they don't make that admission within the seventy or so years of this life, they experience unremitting misery forever with no hope of anything ever changing?

My biggest problem with hell once I became an unChristian wasn't God. It was Christians. Behind their concern for my Lost Soul smol-

---

viii. See what I did there with *Left Behind*, the best-selling series of violence and vengeance-celebrating books that popularized the idea of The Rapture? Although their authors said they portrayed events as the Bible predicted, there is good reason you find those books in the Fiction section of your bookstore or library.

dered the embers of a revenge fantasy. I already mistrusted most Christians who tried to sell me Jesus. They seemed more motivated by their anticipated eternal commission than they were by my fate. But when they started doing the "Sinners in the Hands of an Angry God"[ix] thing, their unspoken, "Or else" overpowered their message.

I recognized each hellfire evangelist as the equivalent of some low-level gangster warning me they'd "hate to see something bad happen" to my business if I didn't pay up to the Boss's protection racket.

And deep down hoping I'd refuse so they could smash up my store.

Or watch the Boss smash me up.

I still get that vibe when some Christians talk about the kinds of folks they believe deserve the fires of hell, particularly those "sinners" who make them the most uncomfortable (LGBTQ folks anyone?) and therefore merit the worst punishment.

The gleeful anticipation of coming vengeance pervades their supposed compassion. "If you don't listen to me you can keep having fun now but YOU'LL GET YOURS in the end. And while I'm enjoying Paradise you'll be burning and burning and burning . . ."

Insert diabolical laugh here.

It's sadistic.

I didn't want anything to do with people like that.

I didn't want anything to do with a God like that.

I still don't.

---

ix. "Sinners in the Hands of an Angry God" was a 1741 sermon that has slammed centuries of listeners and readers with the threat of being thrown into an awful hell by a terrifying God. I read American Great Awakening preacher Jonathon Edwards' sermon in school years ago, but have never shed the image of the sinner as a spider being held over a flame by God Almightily Pissed Off.

16

Forbidden Brownies

I worked for seven years as a Juvenile Probation Officer. So many of the delinquent young people I encountered had addiction issues that I started taking substance abuse counseling courses. One of them was taught by a pharmacist.

At the start of the first class, he said, "I'm going to tell you the secret of why people use drugs."

We leaned forward, expecting enlightenment about endorphins and chemical receptors, something pharmaceutical.

He said, "Because they work."

If drugs didn't make you feel better, at least for a while, they wouldn't be a problem.

If sin wasn't pleasurable, it wouldn't be a problem.

Messed up people who keep on messing up.

That's who we are.

That's who I am.

———

Once upon a time, my mom made the most amazing brownies. When they were cooking the whole house smelled like a big ol' Hershey's Bar. My mouth watered in Pavlovian anticipation of the timer's "DING!" Just a few minutes to cool, and then . . . chocolate nirvana!

I hovered nearby and waited to hear just how long I would have to wait.

Mom picked up her purse. Then she uttered some of the saddest words I knew.

"Don't touch these. I'm taking them to work tomorrow."

She walked out the door, but turned around and added, "There's plenty of other good stuff for you to snack on."

———

Once upon a time, God placed Adam and Eve in the Garden of Eden. They had everything they would ever need. More than that, they had all they could ever want.

Almost.

God only gave them one rule: "Don't eat fruit from the Tree of the Knowledge of Good and Evil. You'll die if you do."

There was plenty of other good stuff for them to snack on.

At some point after that, temptation came to them in the form of a snake. The writer of Genesis doesn't tell us how long Adam and Eve were in the garden before this happened. My guess is if God made the rule in the morning, they were tempted to break it that afternoon. That's human nature for you.

Tempter-snake asked Eve, "Did God really say you couldn't eat any fruit?" Eve answered, "We can eat anything but the fruit from that one tree. God will kill us if we eat it."

———

Soon after my mom left, my friend Dustin (name changed to protect the not-so-innocent) stopped by. The sweet aroma hit him as soon as he walked in the door.

"Brownies!"

The promise of cocoa ecstasy drew him to them.

"Let's have some!"

"We can't. My mom says they're for work."

"Your mom never lets you have anything."

"There's some Pop-Tarts in the pantry. And Chips Ahoy! Anything else is yours. Mom will kill me if we get into those brownies."

"Your mom just wants to keep all the good stuff for herself and her friends!"

———

"You're not going to die if you eat that fruit," Tempter-snake hissed. "God just doesn't want you to be like God. God wants to keep all the good and evil knowledge to Himself[i]. The Man wants to keep you down. He knows if you eat it you'll be on His level."

Eve took another peek at the fruit on the taboo tree. It looked so tasty! And good and evil? She had no idea what that meant but why shouldn't she and Adam know everything God knows?

So she reached out to the tree. She plucked one of the succulent fruits from its branch.

She took a bite.

———

Dustin spoke truth. Mom was just being selfish. I had as much right to those brownies as she did. They looked and smelled so yummy.

I grabbed a knife.

I carefully cut two brownie squares. I gave one to Dustin.

We bit into the cakey chocolate goodness.

———

Eve passed the fruit to Adam. It dripped sweet sticky juice as she passed it to him.

Adam was right there all the time. He was just as culpable as Eve. Maybe even guiltier, or at least more smarmy, as he waited to see what would happen to Eve before he ate. He certainly didn't try to stop her.

Tempter-snake got out of there quick.

Adam and Eve knew right away they had messed up. They felt some new feelings.

Embarrassment warmed their cheeks.

Guilt weighed on their chests.

Then they heard God coming. What had always before been a sweet anticipation became a new sensation. It wasn't just the bit of fruit in their bellies that made their stomachs turn.

They felt fear for the first time.

As ridiculous as it was, they tried to hide from God in the lushness of the garden.

"Where are you?" God called out.

Of course, God knew the answer.

———

i. Of course tempter-snake would use gendered language for God.

We heard Mom's car pull into the driveway. Without a word, Dustin was out the door.

I fled to my room. I shut the door behind me. I covered my ears with headphones and tried to lose myself in Pink Floyd's *Wish You Were Here*.

My mom knocked. "Are you in there?"

Of course, Mom knew the answer.

———

Adam peeked out of the underbrush. "Here I am. I heard you coming. But I was naked so I hid."

"WHO TOLD YOU THAT YOU WERE NAKED?"

Nudity had never been an issue before. There had been no guilt to cover.

"Did you eat from that tree I told you not to touch?"

"It was the woman . . . The woman you made to be with me. She gave it to me and I ate it."

You may think Adam was blaming Eve, but hear what he said again. "The woman you made . . ."

Adam indicted God.

———

"Oh. Hi Mom." I nonchalantly peeled off my headphones. "I came in here because I didn't want to get blamed for the brownies getting eaten."

"And who ate them, gremlins?"

"Look, Mom. You did such a great job making those brownies. They smelled soooo good. I couldn't help it. You never should have left them there. You know I couldn't resist!"

"So it's my fault?"

"Dustin. It was Dustin's idea. Dustin made me."

———

God asked Eve what happened.

"The devil made me do it," Eve answered.

———

Neither God nor my mom bought the excuses or the deflections of blame. Adam, Eve, and I were all punished.

But we were also forgiven, and neither God nor my mom stopped loving their children.

We are loved, even though these stories tell the truth of who we are.

Don't get caught up in whether Adam and Eve were literal people who literally lived in a garden and literally got kicked out.

This is our story.

This is my story.

I am messed up.

I keep messing up.

I need to be cleaned up.

My relationship with God and with other people needs to be reset, and not just once.

I repeat this story over and over again.

It took me a long time to realize that God never stops loving me.

Even though these stories tell the truth of who I am.

17

Kid Preacher
(Seed Planter Mary)

My faith's last gasp happened the summer after eighth grade. On Sunday mornings, I made everyone in the family as miserable as I could with my not-so-passive resistance. Often I ended up left behind with a list of chores to accomplish as Mom, Dad, and my sister drove off to worship.

I didn't have friends at Lakewood Presbyterian, the church we attended in Jacksonville. Nobody there my age went to my school, and I was still mostly socially inept. I either sat sullenly through Sunday School or asked questions the teachers just weren't trained to answer.

Being a nerd, science/Bible contradictions were my specialty.

"If the sun wasn't created until Day Three, how could there be Days One and Two?"

"How can the sun stand still in that story in Joshua? That would mean the earth would stop rotating, and there would be earthquakes and tidal waves and worse. Or did they mean the sun literally stopped because the people who wrote the Bible thought the sun goes around the earth?"

"If the Bible says all the animals were wiped out during the flood, what about animals that live in the sea? If they got killed because of all the fresh water, did Noah have aquariums on the ark?"

Sometimes I would fall back on the old favorites:

"Who did Adam and Eve's sons marry?"

"If God can do anything, can God make a rock so heavy God couldn't pick it up?"

I really wasn't looking for answers. I was just trying to cause trouble and share my angst.

I never asked my real questions. Nobody else seemed to be struggling with faith the way I was. Or at least nobody was willing to admit it.

There's a lot of peer pressure in most churches to exhibit consistent faith lest others think there is something wrong with you. That same pressure suppresses questions and discussions about doubts.

I loved asking questions and learning things. The message I got was that church was the last place you wanted to do either of those.

There were, as we have seen, seed-planting exceptions.

I encountered Mary Baine Rudolph (definitely her real name) during eighth grade. I remember her as a woman in her mid-sixties or so, with the bearing and dignity of someone well off financially. She volunteered in youth ministry, and because I had long ago stopped participating in youth group I didn't have any formal connection with her. On those Sundays I was in church, she made sure to check in with me and have as much of a discussion as I was willing to risk.

She was different than other adults. She listened to what I had to say. She responded with questions for clarification, not correction. She didn't try to force me to agree with anything. She didn't give me a hard time for my questions or for my sporadic attendance.

Mary Baine Rudolph planted seeds not because she was open to my questions, but because she was open to me.

One spring Sunday she brought up a trip some of the youth were taking that summer. There was going to be a huge gathering of high school Presbyterians at a retreat center in the mountains of North Carolina. She thought I should go.

I looked at the pamphlet she handed me and pointed out you were supposed to have finished at least ninth grade to participate.

"Who would know?" she answered. "You need to go."

I trusted her. So I went.

There were some cool parts of the gathering. I met some preachers who weren't middle-aged white men, or at least didn't act like they were. One minister-friend of Mary Baine Rudolph's hugged everyone he met. That was weird, but seemed right for this tie-died clad Grizzly-Adams-bearded pastor. Some of the speakers and breakout sessions focused on social issues, which surprised me.

One evening we watched and discussed *A Man for All Seasons*. Lots of the young people fell asleep. I was enthralled by the battle of wills between Sir Thomas More and Henry VIII. Even then I loved classic film and history.[i]

But I was constantly uncomfortable knowing I wasn't supposed to be there. I was afraid any minute someone would ask me what grade I was in and I'd be asked to leave.

I was also painfully aware of being the youngest in the group from my church. I roomed with three high school guys, and one evening they had a bunch of girls in the room. Nothing happened, but it was unsettling. Girls still kind of scared me.

Another night my oldest roommate broke out some pot and sat on the window ledge smoking it. So the first time I ever encountered illegal drugs was at a church conference.

I left the room.

I ended up in the lobby where a couple of our chaperones (not Mary Baine Rudolph) were watching Johnny Carson. "Why aren't you in bed?"

"You know how Sam is." My pot-smoking roommate could be obnoxious.

"You just have to give him a chance. Get back to your room."[ii]

So I did. But I took the looooong way and by the time I got back Sam was in bed.

I made it through without being expelled for being born too late.

When we got back home, Mary Baine Rudolph wanted us to lead a Sunday morning worship service based on our experiences.

Someone would have to preach.

I don't know how she convinced me, and I barely remember the service, but thanks to Mary Baine Rudolph I preached my first ever sermon that summer after eighth grade.

---

i. For your game show preparation, *A Man for All Seasons* won the 1967 Academy Award for Best Picture, and five other Oscars including Best Actor for Paul Scofield. I had never heard of him. Robert Shaw, on the other hand, who was nominated for Best Supporting Actor, I definitely recognized as the ship captain eaten by the shark in *Jaws*.

ii. I include this detail for anyone who might chaperone a youth trip now. Always ask why someone is not comfortable being in their own room. Or at least trust they have a good reason and give them some space.

Did she know something I wouldn't until more than twenty years later?

A few years ago I started thinking about Mary Baine Rudolph. I thought it would be great to find her and thank her and let her know just how those seeds she planted had grown.

When I Googled her, I found out she had written quite a few books about communicating faith, especially to young people.

Then I found her obituary. Mary Baine Rudolph died in 2009. Here's a line from that remembrance:

"Mrs. Rudolph dedicated her life to Christian education and mission work within the Presbyterian Church and to her family."

I look forward to seeing Mary Baine Rudolph again.

18

The Humane Society

In my memory, he looks something like Benji[i], the movie star dog of the 1970s. He was a scraggily ball of gray, brown, and white fur with big brown saucer eyes. This "Benji" was like that, but he had a little more grey on him, and his eyes were wiser.

I hoped not wise enough to know what was happening to him.

What I was doing to him.

I clearly remember his expression the last time I saw him.

The last time he saw anybody.

He'd been brought to the Humane Society that day by a guy who looked like a grandpa out of Central Casting.[ii] I remember him as sort of an older model Jimmy Stewart. He was rail thin, but the way his clothes hung on him gave away that he used to be stouter. He walked with a slight bow and his hair was neatly combed over.

I remember Benji's owner's eyes, too.

They were rimmed with red.

The old dude had been weeping.

He ambled up to the counter in the Jacksonville Humane Soci-

---

i. Benji was originally played by a dog named Higgins, who also appeared in *Petticoat Junction* and in one of my all-time favorite TV comedies, *Green Acres*. (Those two shows, along with *The Beverly Hillbillies*, took place in the same fictional television reality. Country Store owner Sam Drucker is the nexus of the three.)

ii. Central Casting is an actual company formed in 1925 to supply and pay extras for the growing film industry in California. The phrase "out of Central Casting" originates in the firm's ability to provide actors and actresses who looked like the stereotypical perception of the roles they filled.

ety Receiving Building where I was volunteering that sunny Sunday morning. I loved animals, but this gig was also part of my strategy to get out of going to church. The Humane Society needed me on weekends, and rather than continue the weekly battle that raged for several years, my dad relented on the church attendance requirement because I was "doing good."

Fifteen years old and I was alone at the Receiving counter when Benji and Grandpa came in. I'd been volunteering long enough to know that older dogs just didn't get adopted. And there wasn't room to house them indefinitely.

But this dog . . . this teary older dude . . . they were different.

He was different than the usual folks who dropped off their regular litters of kittens or puppies they couldn't get rid of. I'd been numbed by the uncaring (stupid) folks who didn't seem to know where baby animals came from or how to stop them from coming. I became a "Spay and Neuter Your Pets" evangelist, for all the good it did.[iii]

But this guy and his pooch pierced the armor I'd acquired in the months I'd served behind the Receiving counter.

Grandpa plopped Benji up on the counter. He gave the dog's head a pat.

"I just can't take care of Benji anymore like he deserves. He's been a great pal these last twelve years, but I don't have the energy anymore." Then he raised his gaze to meet my jaded eyes.

"You'll find a good home for him, won't you?"

"We'll certainly see what we can do. You have to fill out this form."

I handed him a half sheet of yellow cardstock, with spaces for his name, address, all the usual stuff. There was also room for information about his dog for any future owners. That part was usually a waste of time considering the huge disparity between the animals coming in my Receiving door versus those leaving through Adoption next door. In a busy summer weekend we might take in 200 animals . . . and adopt out 14.

The vital part of the form was the back. It was blank. If I wrote "Adopt" on the back of the form, it was a ticket to the spacious display cages next door where families could fall in love with a dog or cat and

---

iii. Spay and neuter your pets.

take it home for a lifetime of care and companionship.

If I turned the form over and scrawled (and it was always scrawled, as if it were one letter) "EU," it was a ticket to a lifetime of . . .

Less than an hour.

A little longer on weekdays when animals came in less frequently and it took more time to fill up the EU cage.

EU stood for "euthanasia," and it didn't mean the dog or cat was going to live with a kid in Japan.

So Grandpa handed me the card with his information and stuff about how Benji was housetrained and good with kids and just the greatest all-around canine you could ever know.

"We'll do what we can." That part was true.

"I'm sure someone would love to give Benji a good home." That part was not.

I think he knew. The old guy, I mean. I realize this now looking back.

I thought I was handling him like a pro.

We were really just dancing a dance, avoiding the truth.

They'd both gone and committed the unforgivable sin of getting old. Grandpa got too old to care for a dog. Benji got too old to start over.

And, thinking about it now, Grandpa must not have had anyone to help him out. He'd not just gotten old, he'd gotten old alone.

And now his one friend . . .

"Goodbye, boy." He stroked the dog's tousled fur one last time then handed him to me.

Then the old guy was gone.

There I was with Benji. Just him and me.

And the Card.

When I started volunteering at the Humane Society six months before, I had agonized over the life or death decisions I had to make at the Receiving counter.

Lately, not so much.

But as I held Benji and watched the worn out man drive away in his worn out sedan, I really didn't know what I was going to do.

I knew if I wrote "Adopt" on the back of that card, I would hear about it from my friend Monty who recruited me to volunteer. He would ask me how the hell I expected an old dog to get adopted when there were more puppies and younger housebroken dogs than we could adopt out.

Also, I wouldn't be doing my job. I needed to get the unwanted animals out of the way so the Chosen could get food and care and attention. It wasn't exactly the job I expected when I first biked out to the Humane Society so I could "help animals." Eventually, though, its logic had won me over.

I walked with Benji to the back room. I could put him in one of the EU cages at the far end of the room, or in one of the adoption cages in front. I put him in a holding cage in the middle, one of the few animals who would be staying in Receiving for a while. Those were usually for dogs and cats being observed for rabies, the pets with concerned owners.

Strays suspected of rabies were immediately euthanized and their heads were removed to be sent to the health department for brain analysis. The heads awaited transport in the same refrigerator where we kept our lunches. Eating my bologna sandwich after it had been in close quarters all morning with a possibly rabid cat head or two was something else to get used to.

At fifteen, I was learning you could get used to a lot.

While I continued to waffle over Benji's fate, I made repeated trips from the Receiving counter to the back room. I checked on Benji each time.

There were only two dogs I ever thought of taking home during my time volunteering at the Humane Society. One was an irresistibly cute Keeshond puppy. The other was Benji.

The Keeshond puppy was adopted the day he came in.

Benji wasn't.

Eventually – I don't know how long but before the end of the day – I decided what to do.

It's funny, out of all the animals I sentenced to death, I remember just one. I think that's how memory works.

The last time I saw him was when I put him in the big cage on wheels that got rolled back to the EU machine. That was when he gave me that look I remember so clearly.

I think he knew.

And now, all these years later, my guts still twist up when I think about Benji and Grandpa. I'm still sure I did the right thing in the context of the situation, but I still grieve that it had to be done.

I grieve even more that I was the one who had to do it.

It was another brick in the wall between me and faith in a "good" God, another step away from the religion in which I had been raised.

Good didn't always win in the real world.

God didn't always win in the real world.

Preachers and Sunday School teachers were liars.

And people, who they told us in church were created in God's image?

They tended to kind of suck.

————

One summer afternoon my friend and I were assigned the dirty chore of digging a grave for a horse who had to be shot. The horse had been rescued from an owner who starved it beyond the hope of recovery. I cursed that shithead with every shovelful of sandy dirt.

I went on a few cruelty investigations. For an adolescent asking questions about the goodness and even existence of God, encountering dogs, cats, and all kinds of other animals beaten bloody and broken or starving or diseased due to neglect, and especially encountering the assholes who owned them, only intensified my interrogation of God.

"Where the hell are You?"

It wasn't just the dramatic episodes of cruelty I observed that contributed to my growing cynicism.

It was the people I met on mundane weekends at the Receiving counter. People who give people a bad name.

Like the young couple who drove up one day in the middle of a steaming southern afternoon. They came in lugging a cardboard box full of kittens, tiny white and black balls of fur blending into the newspaper lining the box. The kittens were cute even with the poop and vomit that clung to their fur. A pink tongue lolled out of every little mouth. They panted like they'd run all the way to the Jacksonville Humane Society from Palatka. The kittens were probably not too far from dying of heat prostration.

The young man set the box on the counter. He said – and read this next line as if spoken by Cletus Spuckler:[iv]

"Our momma cat had her some kittens."

What a surprise! You didn't have your cat spayed and you let her traipse all over the neighborhood and now . . . kittens! Kittens you can't or won't take care of or try to find homes for.

Now, here he was hoping we would take care of his box of problems so he could get back to his life of blissful irresponsibility. The kittens were our headache now.

Then Cletus said what just about everybody said, "I hope y'all can find a home for 'em."

Here's what I didn't say:

"I volunteer here because I care about animals, but what I 'get' to do after hosing dog shit out of kennels is to stand here all Saturday and Sunday to take in dogs and cats from people like you who are too lazy or stupid or apathetic to keep their pets from reproducing. I'm in Middle School, and I've been given life or death power. Guess which one your already-almost-dead kittens are going to get?"

This is what I did say:

"They're really panting."

"Yeah, I don't know why in the world that's goin' on. They were fine when we left."

"Maybe because it's almost 100 degrees outside and you brought them here IN YOUR TRUNK! Your CLOSED UP TRUNK that I saw you take them out of in the parking lot. And you CAN'T UN-DERSTAND why they're panting?!"

I didn't say that, either.

Remember, I was just a kid.

I hope you can see why volunteering at the Humane Society fertil-ized my cynicism. For a kid growing up in the cocoon of a suburban family, the capacity of human beings for sadism by omission or com-mission was shocking.

———

One of the services provided by the Jacksonville Humane Society was having someone on call around the clock to go and pick up an-imals in distress with no owners around. Mostly this meant driving

---

iv. Cletus - full name Cletus Del Roy Spuckler - is the hillbilly, aka "Slack Jawed Yokel," character on "The Simpsons."

the Humane Society van out to pick up suffering stray dogs hit by cars and taking them back to Headquarters, then putting them out of their misery.

Occasionally my friend Monty and I would hang out for the evening with the on-call guy hoping the phone would ring so we could ride along. Mike was a young adult who did cruelty investigations at the Humane Society in addition to the on-call gig

On quiet nights, we would hang out and talk.

Mike was another seed planter.

Mike was a Christian, and he talked openly about his faith. He gave Monty and I some Bible Study workbook kind of things, whether we wanted them or not.

I actually completed some of the workbook he gave me. Maybe I was hoping some intellectual engagement could restore my fading faith.

It didn't.

Neither did conversations with Mike, who stayed strong in his Christian conviction in spite of the stuff (and people) he dealt with at the Humane Society. Mike arrived at the Humane Society shortly before I left. My momentum away from faith and away from God at that point was just too strong to be arrested by one genuine Christian.

But . . . Mike was indeed a Seed Planter.

There's no way Mike knows that I eventually became a Christian and a pastor.

Maybe he'll read this book and say, "Hey! That was me."

That would be cool.

Mike planted seeds of faith by sharing his. Even in the face of my questions and sometimes overt hostility, he continued to talk about the difference following Jesus made in his life.

Mike and the other seed planters did not beat me over the head with Bible verses and condemnation for my questions and unbelief. They listened more than they talked and at least acted like they respected and cared about my objections.

When they took my doubts seriously they took me seriously.

Most Christians I encountered who endeavored to evangelize pelted me with their faith as if throwing down seeds as hard as they could onto untilled ground.

I'm sure they believed they were following General Jesus' orders ("Onward Christian Soldiers!") and that if their conversion incursion failed it was my fault for being "stony soil."[v]

It was their supposed seeds that were the stones. Often they hurt.

———

I forget why I was handling the cat, but for some reason I opened its cage and it sunk its teeth into the back of my hand – hard. That was bad enough, but then it ran out of the building and into the woods behind the Humane Society.

The pain was bad. The embarrassment of mishandling the cat was worse. But the worst by far was there was no way to test the cat for rabies.

Some Humane Society administrator asked me if I wanted to get rabies shots "just in case." I'd heard about the series of thick needles in your stomach and didn't want to go through that. It was a different time back then as my parents were never consulted about possible treatment. I don't think I ever told them about the bite because I was afraid they'd make me stop going, which would have been tragic because the cat bite happened about the time I developed a miserable unrequited crush on another young volunteer.

I was in ninth grade and spent most of my lunches that school year in the library. The food at school sucked and I usually forgot to bring lunch from home because I was running out the door to the bus at the absolute last minute.

Usually I spent those library lunches reading Sports Illustrated (the Swimsuit Edition was particularly educational) or some other magazine. After the cat incident I used a few lunchtimes to do in-depth medical research, at least as in-depth as you could in a middle school[vi] library.

Young folks, in the mid-70s you couldn't hop on the internet and search WebMD. There was no Google, only googol, a very big number that impressed nerds like me and my friends.[vii]

———

v. In Matthew 13:1-23, Mark 4:1-20, and Luke 8:1-15, Jesus tells the Parable of the Four Soils, each representing how the Gospel might be received.

vi. In Jacksonville back then, Middle School was eighth and ninth grade. High School was tenth through twelfth.

vii. A googol, of course, is a one with a hundred zeroes. Less well-known but even more

I was stuck with whatever books were at hand.

There was enough information available to provoke worry. I learned rabies has a six to twelve month incubation period.

It was a long year.

During some idle times I could feel something sinister growing within me, like *The Tingler* in the old Vincent Price horror flick.[viii]

When I remembered the cat bite (which thankfully happened less and less often as the year progressed), I felt around my lips or looked in the mirror to see if I'd started foaming at the mouth yet.

I found out rabies is also known as *hydrophobia* (fear of water) because your throat swells up and it becomes agonizing to drink until you refuse to take in liquids.

Any hint of a sore throat – real or imagined – during that year brought my mind right back to the moment when that not-so-cute kitty dug its teeth into my hand. I would do scientific tests by pouring a glass of water then making sure I could drink it as easily as I had the week or month before. I just wanted to be prepared for what might be coming.

You know what I never thought to do?

Pray.

When I was afraid I reached out for information, and not for God.

There was a definite disconnect between my 'real life' and all those Sundays I had spent in church.

---

impressive (again, to nerds like me and my friends) is the googol-plex, which is a googol times a googol. (I was going to end that sentence with an exclamation point but that kind of excitement, while an accurate expression of my middle school mentality, is just embarrassing now. Even if it is still accurate.)

viii. *The Tingler* scared the crap out of me when I saw it on TV one afternoon when I was in elementary school. It's a 1959 movie about a scientist (Price) who discovers a worm-thing that grows on your spine when you're afraid. It's the "tingle" of fear. A scream kills the tingler, but he figured out if he could prevent someone from screaming the tingler would grow to humongous size. Then one got loose . . . What was that tingle I felt in my spine? When *The Tingler* was released in theaters, some seats were wired with vibrators on their backs that were activated when the tingler was on the loose. Good thing I didn't see it in the theater. Fortunately I wasn't born yet in 1959.

<u>19</u>

The Mystery Dance

Being too smart for God, the sexual part of my journey is characterized by making up my own rules and rationalizing my less than honorable choices.

In my defense, I was pretty much on my own. The schools I attended never offered any kind of sex education. Sex wasn't talked about or even mentioned in church. Maybe after I fled Youth Group in middle school it was covered, but I missed out if it was.

Churches that wait until after middle school to initiate discussions about sex with their young people are missing out as well. They squander any chance to effectively influence young people about intimacy.

Such churches abstain from influence in a culture that, much more now than when I was growing up, portrays sex as an opportunity for unbridled *self*-gratification, sort of masturbation with a partner.

Or lots of partners over time.

The church has been so afraid of young people – particularly girls – becoming sexually active it has focused solely on "purity" at the expense of discussion about healthy relationships. Christianity is at its heart relational, and the church has a lot to say about all kinds of relationships.

Many Christian leaders have found it easier to chastise young women for the way they dress that supposedly entices young men who are purportedly unable to control themselves than to teach those young men concepts like consent.

The Christian purity movement is a culture of shame. In one purity curriculum exercise, an unwrapped Hershey's Kiss is passed around so everyone touches it. Now it has everyone's germs on it! "Who wants to eat it now?"

Other exercises involve chewed-up gum or a used toothbrush.

Can you imagine how that would make a young woman feel who has been sexually abused? Or a young woman who made a coerced decision she now regrets?

The lessons are about the "purity" of young women, rarely young men.

Perhaps we in the church need to admit the worst thing that could happen is not that a girl might lose her virginity, but rather that she would be manipulated, used, or raped. Instead of enhancing the tantalizing mystery of sex by making it some sort of ultimate taboo, the church should focus on empowering young people – especially young women – to appreciate themselves as God's creation, loved unconditionally by the God who formed them.

Maybe the church could even help young women appreciate their bodies, in all their variety, independent of male opinion and approval.

Don't get me started on how the church has shamed and ostracized those whose sexuality and gender don't conform to being "normal."

But for now, back to my own sordid sexual story.

Actually, it's not that sordid.

Like I said, there was no guidance about sex from the school or church. And very little at home.

My parents never had The Talk with me. They gave me a book about the mechanics of baby-making when I was about thirteen, kind of the way you'd give a kid interested in carpentry a book about woodworking.

But for me, it was more like getting the owner's manual to a car I'd already owned for a while.

And driven for a few miles.

But not yet with passengers.

The Talk is a myth anyway. Kids don't need The Talk; they need Ongoing Conversation about choices and limits and consequences and especially consent and agency over their bodies.

The message I did get about sex was pretty much "Don't get anyone pregnant and don't get any diseases." (We're not going to tell you exactly what those diseases might be. But parts might fall off.)

I assume my parents would rather I waited until I was married or at least out of the house to put anything in the owner's manual into practice. But they never said anything one way or the other.

The single mother of a middle school friend of mine gave him a much more interesting book to read – *Everything You Always Wanted to Know about Sex (But Were Afraid to Ask)* by Dr. David Rueben. The book instantly intrigued me with its sunny yellow cover and subtitle that summed up my situation perfectly.

I was afraid to ask *anything* about sex.

I consumed the book in just a few visits to my friend's house. I still get a little warm when I remember reading Dr. Reuben's description of what happened to bodies during orgasm.

The book opened up a whole new world of stuff I had no idea about like *female* orgasm and The Question of the Century:

"What is the average size of the penis?"

Besides member-measuring, I didn't rush out to try any of the stuff I read in that book. In seventh grade I had no willing partners and would have been terrified if I did. But that book expanded my horizons for the future. Reading it was like when we studied about Greece. I knew there was no way I was going to get there soon, but by golly I was going to make the trip someday!

Ultimately, *Everything You Always Wanted to Know about Sex (But Were Afraid to Ask)* was just another, flashier, owner's manual. It was as incomplete as the one my parents gave me. There was nothing about when or how to apply the brakes once you got going. There was nothing about empathy for the person with whom you did all this wonderful stuff besides making them feel good physically.

I'm glad I never tried some of Dr. Reuben's "scientific" birth control methods – Coca-Cola douches after sex for women, Saran Wrap for guys if there were no condoms available.[i] I probably would have violated the "Don't get anyone pregnant" rule if I had. I imagine it is awfully difficult to apply Saran Wrap in a way that is impervious to bacteria.

Other friends ran afoul of both rules. I knew guys who participated in a number of abortions. Now *that* scared me. The whole idea of going with a girl to a clinic made me extra careful once I did start putting that owner's manual into practice.

---

i. Kids, don't try this at home!

As careful as I was, there would be times when I rejoiced when a girlfriend's period started. Yes, I did some praying in those situations (just in case) and now can say only by the grace of God I did not have to deal with being a teenage sperm donor.

Sex was a mix of mystery[ii], fear, and pleasure. As long as I didn't violate the Two Rules, and I didn't get caught by girlfriends' parents, I was good. I rationalized that as long as I was careful, I could have as much "fun" as I wanted.

At least as much as I could get away with.

It was all about me and what I wanted.

What did I want? To feel good and maybe "manly" and like I was keeping up with other guys.

Remember that pharmacist who said people use drugs because they "work."

Sex "worked" for me in meeting those primal and selfish wants I aimed to satisfy.

It might sound more sympathetic to say I was looking for love. But I've already made it clear that I always knew I was loved by my parents. It's not as simple as parenting experts make it sound: *Just let your kids know they are loved and they won't need to be sexually active.*

Maybe I didn't *need* to dance the "Mystery Dance," but I sure *wanted* to. Like most adolescents, I was not adept at distinguishing between needs and wants.

Maybe the church could help young people discern that difference if it was serious about helping them make informed and healthy choices about sex.

I could have used that guidance. Although I made an A in mathematical calculus, I sucked at moral calculus.

I rationalized selfish desires and acted on them whenever I could.

I'm not going to do a celibacy lecture here because obviously that would be hypocritical. But what I wish I had known that wasn't in the owner's manual – or in Dr. Reuben's book – is this:

Intimacy is a beautiful gift from God.

---

ii. "The Mystery Dance" by Elvis Costello is probably the best expression of confused male teenage sexuality ever. (I'm listening to it as I write this.)

20

Secret Messages

I heard rumors of a thing called Cable Television. Instead of six stale, sometimes snowy, stations, dozens of channels clearly cascaded through a coax connection.

Cable Television wired our neighborhood my senior year of high school. I was not above begging my parents to subscribe. My sales pitch focused on the educational channels. Back then TLC still stood for The Learning Channel and Discovery actually helped viewers discover science and history. A&E's programming reflected the "arts" the "A" stood for. This was long before the devolution of most "educational" programming into fonts of lowest common denominator reality and tabloid TV.

I didn't know if my budget-conscious parents would pay for something that had always been a free frivolity.

But they did!

Cable Television magically transformed our twenty-seven-inch color console television into a Box of Wonders.

Movies without commercial interruption! Movies without censorship! 24/7 Sports! I hadn't even known I wanted to watch the NBA Draft until we got ESPN!

Back then, ESPN showed a lot of Australian Rules Football. My friends and I watched hours of the exotic sport without ever really figuring out the Australian rules.

Cable Television provided hours of enjoyment, excitement, titillation, and often just empty mesmerization.

It also provided potent ammunition for blowing up my faith.

I know what some of you folks are thinking: I was corrupted by cable's carnal content[i].

Nope.

The last embers of my faith were doused by *PTL*, not HBO.

PTL stood for "Praise the Lord." Every afternoon Jim and Tammy Bakker's *The PTL Club* live television extravaganza entered my living room.

Many days I watched *Match Game*. The celebrity game show seemed like a half-hour peek through a window into adulthood. That is, a fantasy rendering of adulthood as a non-stop cocktail party where everyone was witty and sarcastic and risqué.

But once we got Cable Television, *The PTL Club* gave *Match Game* stiff competition for my after school hours. It was a ninety-minute descent into a bizzaro world Tonight Show.

On *The Tonight Show*, Ed McMahon introduced Johnny Carson. Ed served as Johnny's faithful sidekick who sat on a couch next to Johnny's desk and chuckled at all his jokes.

On the *PTL Club*, Jim Bakker was introduced by a jocular jowly fellow who looked how Ed McMahon might've turned out if he'd consumed lots of biscuits and gravy instead of Budweiser. The announcer, nicknamed "Tranny" (really!) and Jim Bakker shared sort of a desk that had a ridge around the front giving it the appearance of a two-man pulpit. Tranny threw in some "Amens" and heartfelt exclamations of "Yessss" along with the chuckles.

Johnny Carson looked and acted the paragon of suave. He exuded an LA cool that was laid back, never really bothered by anything. He could have been a model for the eponymous suits he wore.

Jim Bakker was no one's idea of cool. He never seemed comfortable on television or even in his own skin. His laughs were nervous. He was a little guy and looked like he could have been one of the puppets on the children's show he hosted with Tammy before *The PTL Club*.

The homey set of Jim Bakker's show invoked the impression you had been invited over to the Bakker's garishly gilded mansion for the afternoon. Behind him were gaudily treated windows with "trees"

---

i. I realize there's an inordinate amount alliteration so far in this chapter. Sometimes I can't control it – alliteration flows like a florid flooded flume. (I'll tone it down some.)

visible through them.

Guests on *The PTL Club* shared stories from their personal lives and their adventures in the evangelism industry.

They also sang. Each episode showcased Tammy's talents, the format designed to demonstrate the superiority of her singing. She was always the featured performer and the guests were just the opening acts.

Jim Bakker began each show with a comical (to my friends and me) pitch for viewers to send him money in the name of JEEEE-zus. A bank of phone operators sat in several tiers off to his right. It had the look of a perpetual charity telethon.

It was.

The Bakkers were the charity.

Jim and Tammy were always "just a little behind" on their bills, but nothing a generous Love Offering couldn't fix.

If you sacrificially donated to Jim and Tammy, God would surely bless you real good. God worked on the "you scratch my back, I'll scratch yours" principle.

God liked His[ii] back scratched with fifties and hundreds and big checks made out to *The PTL Club*.

Jim and Tammy were proponents of the Prosperity Gospel.

God wants you to be rich! God wants to stop those debt collectors that have been driving you crazy with their calls. God wants you to move into the mansion in which God planned for you to dwell! God wants you to tell those doctors, "The Holy Spirit is the only medicine I need."

A-ME-IN![iii]

Yesssss!

God wants to prosper you. God wants *Your Best Life Now*.[iv] God wants it for you soooo bad!

But God can't give it to you.

Do you know why?

You.

---

ii. God was singularly male for these folks.

iii. These folks managed to put three syllables into "amen."

iv. Actual book title by the smoothest Prosperity Gospel preacher of them all, Smilin' Joel Osteen.

You are keeping God from blessing you with the prosperity God wants for you.

(Who knew you were more powerful than God?)

All you've got to do to clear up God's consecration constipation is to apply the spiritual ex-lax of faith.

You just gotta believe!

What is the surest sign of faith that will remind God of the combination to the Eternal Safe?

A sacrificial Love Offering to the prosperity preacher!

Here's something seventeen-year-old budding atheist me shares with fifty-something-year-old pastor me:

We both know the Prosperity Gospel is bullshit.

Now I use the theological word "heretical" instead of invoking bovine excrement[v], but it means the same thing.

I didn't have the theological chops to discredit the "Name It and Claim It" grifters. But my parents had read me stories about lamps that produced wish-granting genies when rubbed.

I knew they were fairy tales.

Jim Bakker and his ilk made God into the genie. "Faith" rubbed the lamp.

Adolescents excel at spotting fakes and charlatans. My cynicism enhanced that natural acumen.

My friends and I were on to Jim and Tammy long before their *PTL* empire fell apart in financial and sexual scandal. Jim couldn't get out of jail by rubbing that proverbial lamp.[vi]

---

v. Don't get on me for using scatological language. Martin Luther was a master of it – he once described his depression like this: "I am ripe shit, so is the world a great wide asshole; eventually we will part." But mostly he reserved his potty mouth for insults, especially aimed at Satan, like, "Dear Devil . . . I have shat in my pants and breeches; hang them on your neck and wipe your mouth with them." That's the same Devil he advocated chasing away with a fart. And another thing about scatological language – it's in the Bible! Philippians 3:8, cleaned up in the NIV Bible as in all English Scripture, says, "What is more, I consider everything a loss because of the surpassing worth of knowing Christ Jesus my Lord, for whose sake I have lost all things. I consider them garbage, that I may gain Christ." The word translated "garbage" in polite English Bibles is *scubala* in the original Greek. When Paul (remember him?) wrote that, he did not mean "garbage." The word means, let's be a little less polite, "dung."

vi. But he is still selling those lamps. Since his parole, Bakker has traded the Prosperity Gospel for End Times fear-mongering. It's still working for him as a business plan; he'll sell you a bucket of survival food if you call the 800 number at the bottom of your screen and make

We didn't need to wait for their fall from grace to know what was up. We watched *The PTL Club* because it so blatantly bilked its viewers. It was a daily opportunity to feel superior, to both despise the Bakkers' ethics and to work up a little schadenfreude[vii] for the folks we considered too stupid to know it was all a long con.

I didn't consider the people preyed upon by the Bakkers and other purveyors of the Prosperity Gospel might be desperate rather than stupid.

Judgment is always easier than empathy, especially for adolescents. Too many adults – and far too many Christians – never overcome their propensity for blaming victims rather than trying to walk in their shoes.

But, my goodness, *The PTL Club* confirmed my every inkling that I was too smart for God. The show not only ascended to the heights of hokeyness, but actively promoted ignorance. Evolution was evil. The world was created in seven literal days a few thousand years ago. Adam and Eve were literal people who rode around on dinosaurs.[viii]

Based on my experience and what I saw on Cable Television, I concluded you had to reject science to be a Christian.

The type of Christianity with which I was acquainted could not bear scientific inquiry.

If God could not withstand rational investigation, I had no use for God.

———

I've got to share with you the most ridiculous thing I saw on *The PTL Club*.

It may seem small, even insignificant, but it shoved me mightily onward in the direction I was already heading.

Away from the church. Away from faith.

One day one of my favorite bands appeared on *The PTL Club*.

Not the band, exactly, but their music.

Backwards.

That afternoon I watched Cable Television with a friend who

---

a Love Offering to his new, post-prison ministry.

vii. Schadenfreude is one of my favorite words; a German noun for which there is no exact English equivalent. It means pleasure derived from someone else's misfortune.

viii. I may be conflating some things in that last sentence.

shared my love of the Electric Light Orchestra.[ix] I switched over to Jim and Tammy in mid-show. Jim was holding up an album cover. It was *Face the Music* by ELO!

What the hell was going on?

Then they played part of the opening track, "Fire on High." It's mostly instrumental, but there's some words spoken backwards at the beginning. That's the part they played. They seemed amazed it wasn't intelligible.

Then they reversed it, and a deep voice (Bev Bevan's, the drummer) intoned:

"The music is reversible, but time is not. Turn back. Turn back. Turn back."

Jim turned to the guest on the couch beside his double-pulpit desk. "That's amazing! I can hear the secret message!"

The guest said he'd played lots of demon rock and roll records backwards.

What a job!

He claimed to have found all kinds of secret messages implanted by the Satanic rock and roll musicians. They supposedly wanted kids to worship Satan - without knowing it, I guess, since they couldn't understand the backwards stuff - and commit suicide.

And have sex, which was even worse.

Why did those evil rockers do it?

Because all rock artists are Satan worshippers, obviously.

So this guy explained to the credulous, mouth-agape Jim Bakker about these secret messages. He played a few of them. The backward "messages" were as clear as the "wah wah wah" adults on Charlie Brown animated specials.

If the backward spinner guy told you what it said, you might – might – be able to hear a shadow of it. Like when someone points at a cloud and says, "That looks like a bunny," and you say, "Yeah, I think I can see a bunny there."

Or the Virgin Mary on a piece of toast.

The guy took something ELO did as sort of a joke and made it his

---

ix. Also known as ELO. They are still sort of a guilty pleasure of mine. I'm listening to them – frontwards – as I write this.

evidence that rock and roll contained dangerous Satanic Secret Messages.

My friend and I could not stop laughing.

Then Jim Bakker monetized the moment. He got very serious and kind of scared and addressed the camera directly. "We've got to stop this."

Send money.

We imagined those Love Offerings funding a room filled with men and women sitting at turntables, each wearing headphones. With their left hands they spun record after record backwards on those turntables. With their right hands they diligently recorded all the Secret Satanic Messages they thought they heard.

I did not want to be associated with people like that.

I still don't.

It wasn't just Jim Bakker and *The PTL Club*. That just happened to be on cable television during that after-school/before-dinner time easily filled with channel surfing. The antics of other televangelists – Ernest Angley's "Put your ha-ands on your television screeeen" comes immediately to mind – contributed to my desire to distance myself from Christianity.

Which meant distancing myself from the experience of God and God's love.

————

If I have come across in this chapter as even more sarcastic than usual – even angry – that's because I am pissed off. I felt the anger build as I wrote about these long ago television programs.

Those who would monetize God and profit off vulnerable people who desperately seek God's help are guilty of swindling the very people Jesus prioritized.

They are also culpable for poisoning attitudes toward the church – and the faith – of those outside or on the margins of Christianity.

TV hucksters in preachers' clothing who use religion – who use God – to make a quick buck are as destructive to the Body of Christ as those who spew racist hate in the name of Jesus.

For me, already on the way out the door of the church, the antics of Jim and Tammy Bakker, along with others I encountered on Cable Television, only hastened my departure.

Church must be for weak, stupid people.
God must be for weak, stupid people.

I might not have been the strongest person, but I sure wasn't stupid.

Alabama

21

Crossing the Line

I can pinpoint the moment I first professed atheism.

But . . . can you profess atheism?

Usually, to *profess* is to state that one belongs, or to affirm one agrees with a set of beliefs and practices. When a person is baptized in my church, they (or their parents) are asked to: "Profess your faith in Christ Jesus, reject sin, and confess the faith of the Church, the faith in which we baptize.[i]"

At eighteen, I declared precisely the opposite.

Atheism by definition is all about *un*belief. One doesn't believe in God – not just the Christian God but any God.

That's what I meant when I first declared myself an atheist.

It was my freshman year of college. I was outside my dorm one warm fall Alabama evening sitting on a park bench. A young woman I knew sat down next to me.

I thought she seemed kind of down.

Maybe it was the tears.

I was quite the perceptive young man.

"What's wrong?" I asked.

She needed to vent. She stood in front of me and unloaded. There were lots of things wrong. Most serious was the imminent death of her grandmother. As she verbally handed me each burden, she rocked back and forth.

---

i. Inter-Lutheran Commission on Worship. (1978). Lutheran book of worship. Minneapolis: Augsburg Publishing House. Page 123.

Finally, she reached the end of her lament.

"Wow," I said. I know that doesn't sound like much of a response, but in my defense my one-word reply did acknowledge the overwhelming nature of her troubles. I did not minimize. I did not try to solve her problems by giving advice.

And I did not practice what I call "fisherman listening" which is trying to top the other person's troubles with bigger troubles of your own.

She slumped down on the bench beside me, exhausted.

We were silent for a while. Then she found a second wind and started talking with enthusiasm about God and how He would take care of everything and that her grandmother was in His hands and all we needed to do was believe and pray.

And pray . . .

It took a couple moments of uncomfortable silence, but I realized she was waiting for me to pray.

Huntingdon College[ii], my alma mater in Montgomery, Alabama, is affiliated with the Methodist Church. But the denominational affiliation had nothing to do with my enrollment. I chose Huntingdon because I fell in love with the intimacy of the place[iii] when I attended a Step-Ahead summer program after my junior year of high school. Step-Ahead was an opportunity to get to know what college was like, to live in a dorm, and take two courses for credit. It was six weeks without parents.

I hadn't applied anywhere else in spite of Huntingdon's Christian underpinnings that were, in practice, somewhat muted.

The religious requirements to attend a few Convocations in the chapel each year and the presence of the so-called "God-squad" students who had come to Huntingdon for the religion were just inconveniences to endure.

Or to be made fun of, in the case of the God Squad's naively earnest fresh-faced version of Christianity.

---

ii. Huntingdon's two most famous alumni are Harper Lee, the author of the racial-boundary breaking *To Kill a Mockingbird*, and James Sessions, the US Attorney General who previously failed to be confirmed for a federal judge position because of his history of defending racial boundaries.

iii. When I attended, Huntingdon had fewer than 700 students.

So this young woman stood in front of me, waiting for partnership in prayer.

I had never prayed with anyone in public. The touchy-feeliness of praying with someone made me incredibly uncomfortable.

The biggest obstacle, though, was that I had lost touch with the intended recipient of the prayer.

Praying with that troubled young woman would have been like pretending to talk on a toddler's toy phone. When you're a little child, it's fun. You can imagine someone on the other end and indulge in a full conversation. But for a young adult, especially a self-regarded smart young adult like me, it's just stupid – and embarrassingly puerile – to converse with a piece of plastic that's not connected to anything. Or to anyone.

So I didn't pray.

I didn't say anything.

My friend, pretty perceptive herself, asked this:

"David, you don't believe in God, do you?"

It was a Moment of Decision.

Did I believe in God? I had never been asked. More importantly, I had never confronted *myself* with that question. At least not directly. It was easier – and safer – to just ignore it.

I indulged my doubts. I made fun of those who were sure. I stayed away from church and other Christian manifestations, but my resistance was passive.

It was like the end of a marriage when one spouse asks the other, after months or even years of going through the motions, "Do you still love me?"

The conversation on the Huntingdon bench was sort of a reverse Altar Call.

In Baptist and other similar denominations the preacher ends the sermon by inviting those who "made a decision for Jesus" to get out of their pews and make their way to the front of the church, toward the altar. Different pastors have varied strategies to get folks to respond. I've been in churches where the pastor won't move on until at least one person comes forward, and when someone does eventually make the move you wonder if it's just because they have a lunch reservation or a tee time.

My bench companion wasn't moving until I answered her question. She rephrased it slightly.

"David, do you believe in God?"

"No, I don't."

Lightening did not strike. The earth did not shake open to swallow me. The young woman did not point an accusing finger and shout, "Heretic!"

She wasn't sure what to say. I may have been the first professed atheist she had ever met. Lots of students came to Huntingdon from a homogeneous bubble of white southern gentility.[iv]

I don't remember any more of our conversation. There might not have been any more. There's a good chance we silently went our separate ways, neither of us sure where to go from there.

What had brought me to that point?

If you've been with me this far, you know part of it was my cynical nature. There was plenty in the church to feed my cynicism.

But my primary obstacle to faith was not cynicism itself, but the root of it.

I finally gave voice to what I had determined long ago.

I was too smart for God.

---

iv. There were a few African-American students at Huntingdon, but hardly any social integration. Folks of color weren't enough of a presence to make anyone in power think the homecoming theme one year, "Plantation Memories," complete with a logo reminiscent of the Confederate Battle Flag, might be offensive. I learned the danger of satire that year when the underground newspaper some friends and I started ("Hawk Droppings" – our mascot was a hawk) included a "classified ad" seeking "One black man for public whipping during the Homecoming celebration." That angered the administration as we had intended, but also the Black Student Association, who did not appreciate our privileged sarcasm.

22

How to Chase Away
an UnChristian

Many of the things said by well-meaning believers that were supposed to entice (or terrify) me back into church had the opposite effect of reinforcing my happy existence without God.

Yes, I was mostly happy. Any unhappiness had little or nothing to do with my lack of faith.

Perhaps we should start there, with the assumption that unChristians are miserable.

From the outside, it appears Christians are the ones who are woebegone, who fit H. L. Mencken's definition of puritanism:

"The haunting fear that someone, somewhere may be happy."

The judgmental condemnation emanating from Christians with the biggest microphones (and keyboards) looks nothing like happiness. For them, following Jesus seems a quest for well-being based on establishing superiority over anyone they have decided is not only a lesser being but also damned to hell.

In my experience, the most vocal Christians in my workplaces and social circles were the ones who proclaimed their faith by their sanctimony. The song may say, "They will know we are Christians by our love," but I knew many Christians by their aversion to cursing and drinking and anything having to do with [whispered voice] sex.

Those who seemed concerned about my faith apart from actions that offended them often approached with an attitude of "soul winning" in which I was reduced to nothing more than a mark in an elaborate multi-level marketing scheme.

Listen, Christians. It is obvious when you don't care about a person other than as a potential trophy for your stack of saved souls' scalps. You're not fooling anyone when you are uninterested in empathetic interaction but rather in making a sales pitch.

You're no more genuine than the woman at the Taco Bell drive-thru we often visit. The consistent montone of her "How are you?" makes it obvious that she asks because she's been trained to do so, not because she has any real concern for us.

Christians who turned me off were not interested in relationship, but instead in winning an argument. They wanted to put me in my place, and convince me of my folly.

Not only did they desire to prove their moral superiority, they also wanted to demonstrate their supposedly superior intellect. They believed themselves smarter than atheists and their allies: the evolutionists and the archaeologists and of course the liberal media. Their unspoken message was that I had been taken in by those deceptive forces of Satan and they were just plain wiser than me.

That certainly didn't work!

Neither did their challenges to my integrity:

"You're not really an atheist, are you? I mean, deep down, you really believe, right??"[i]

Some Christians can't conceive of someone going through life without believing in God. So they project their own limited imagination onto those who profess unbelief and figure they are lying or self-deluded. That was not the best way to lead me into a conversation about Jesus.

When I said I didn't believe in God, I didn't believe in God.

Did I have doubts sometimes? Sure. That's when I identified myself as an agnostic rather than an atheist. But an agnostic isn't someone who is hiding a secret faith. An agnostic sees no evidence for God but realizes you can't prove a negative.

One sure way to shut down any conversation is to accuse such a person of being a closet believer.

That accusation is at the root of the failed approaches I wrote about earlier:

---

i. Throughout this chapter, I am bolding the "Ways to Chase Away an UnChristian." That way, Christians who read this can find them easily and NOT SAY THEM!

"You know you're going to hell, don't you?"

Or the Evangelism Explosion question:

"If you died tonight and stood before God and he asked, 'Why should I let you into my heaven,' what would you say?"

If I didn't believe in God – and therefore didn't believe in hell - this was like warning me about bad luck from breaking mirrors or walking under ladders. I was not going to worry about superstition or let it change me. There were plenty of real dangers about which to be concerned.

Read this slowly if you still think threatening an unChristian with hell is a good idea: If I don't believe in something, I am not afraid of it.

The threat of hell and the Evangelism Explosion question are rooted in the faulty belief that deep down unChristians really DO believe in God, and are therefore concerned about what God might do to them after they die. Especially for someone like me who believed he was too smart for God, such an approach is a dud.

As are cute little bumper sticker-appropriate sayings. My favorite was when Christians told me that I was incomplete because **"I had a God-shaped hole."**

Perhaps the best response would have been, "I'll show you mine if you show me yours!"

I'm a Christian now – a pastor even – and that one still mystifies me. I heard it from more than one proselytizer, so it must be a thing. Or at least it was when I was an unChristian.

Apparently the idea of a "God-shaped hole" is often attributed to a guy who could have written a book called *Way, Way Too Smart for God*. Blaise Pascal was a seventeenth century French mathematician, physicist, and eventually a Christian philosopher. Those who want to give the "God-shaped hole" a weighty pedigree will tell you that Pascal wrote about a "God-shaped vacuum[ii]." The reality is that there is a paragraph in his meaty treatise, *Pensées* ("Thoughts"), about an abyss that "can only be filled with an infinite and immutable object, in other

---

ii. I once lost a bet with my grandmother about the spelling of "vacuum." I insisted there was no way it could have two *u*'s. I was wrong, of course. I should have learned more than to spell "vacuum" from that encounter; a lesson about the pomposity of youth and the wisdom of experience would have been helpful, but being wrong left me no less sure of my intellectual superiority. I did not accept defeat easily; I remember checking a dictionary or two when I got home from Grandma's.

words God Himself."

But that wouldn't fit on a bumper sticker.

Besides formulating groundbreaking mathematics and inventing the adding machine, Pascal is also famous for his eponymous wager.[iii] This godly gamble was offered to me fairly often during my unChristian days.

Pascal's Wager is basically this: If you live your life "betting" there is no God and there is one, you're in trouble. If you bet the other way – that God exists – and you are wrong, you are no worse off than you were before.

So, why not live as if God were real?

Blaise's Bet (I like my alliterative name better) only confirmed some of the negative suspicions I had about Christians. I thought most if not all of them were going through the motions of obedience. They didn't really believe in God but, as Mr. Smythe had asserted, they were too scared of what people would think if they didn't. Or they were afraid of what would happen to them after they died and discovered the God in which they couldn't muster faith existed.

The idea of Christian faith – or faith in any deity – seemed so ridiculous that I couldn't see how anyone but the most imbecilic could hold onto it. Even I didn't believe most people could be that stupid.

Blaise's Bet is simply another reduction of Christianity to an eternal insurance policy with Churches as sales branches. Pay up now – with your obedience and your offering and your good works and your church attendance and so on – and hope you collect when you die.

I wasn't going to pay eternity insurance by submitting to some God I didn't believe in, or support some church that perpetuated the corrupt system. To act as if I believed in God when I did not, in case God might be angry at me if God did in fact exist, was intellectually dishonest. And to capitulate to the reasoning of Blaise's Bet would have curtailed what I perceived to be my freedom to act and think as I wished.

Not wanting to follow the rules was not my primary reason for being an unChristian, though.

---

iii. If you're preparing for *Jeopardy!*, Pascal is a good name to know. He comes up fairly often for his wager, but also for his namesake measure of atmospheric pressure. If you remember that "17th century French mathematician" = Pascal, you'll do fine. Oh, and Pascal is also the most popular variety of celery, a fact the show has referenced a few times as well.

Another sure way to cut off conversation was to accuse me of **rejecting God because I just wanted to do what I wanted to do.**

Classifying atheists and agnostics as selfish libertines is neither accurate nor effective as an evangelism strategy. It is a great way to proceed if you want to block any hope of mutually respectful conversation.

Some of the most moral folks I know act with justice and mercy without the aid of religion. I have friends who have been faithfully married for years, who have raised empathetic and compassionate children, but who don't believe in God or especially in religion.

We Christians must get rid of our prejudices about people who don't believe the same as we do. Moral superiority is not a winning posture; others tend not to listen when we pontificate from on high.

The point of sharing your faith in Jesus with someone is not to get them to behave like you want them to behave. If that is your primary goal, you need to get your own faith straight before you start trying to straighten out anyone else.

One evangelism tactic I particularly enjoyed was when a Christian apologist wanted to **debate evolution**.

That's actually just what *I* wanted. If I could turn the conversation into an argument about science, I didn't have to deal with Jesus.

Those young-earth creationists who wanted to tell me about the ark being found on Mount Ararat (you can see it in the satellite picture!) or about caveman dinosaur rodeos (not exactly but that's where my mind went when they talked about dinosaurs and humans coexisting) only widened the divide between me and Christianity. If I had to give up science – and scientific thought – in order to become a Christian, then no thanks.

If forced to choose between Darwin and Jesus, I'd take Darwin. I could see tangible evidence of evolution in the world and in the work of scientists. If I had to believe against all rational data that the universe was only a few thousands (rather than billions) of years old, then count me out.

Either scientists were wrong or God was playing games with us, setting up all the evidence for the big bang and evolution and so on in order to mislead us.

I'm still too smart for that God.

If you're a young earth creationist kind of Christian, we can agree to disagree.

Maybe not, because you probably think I'm hell-bound.

I hope you can see my point here. To debate evolution vs. creationism with an unChristian may make you feel noble and persecuted, like you're fighting the Good Fight against Godless Science, but it is not likely to bring them any closer to faith in Jesus. You give them the impression that we are saved by "correct" belief in what happened 5000 years ago rather than by faith in what happened on the cross and at the empty tomb 2000 years ago.

Occasionally **I would be challenged to prove there is no God**.

Ah ha! They got me with that one!

Of course I couldn't prove there's no God. Nor did I want to. I wasn't trying to convince my Christian interlocutors of anything. They were trying to get me over to their point of view, so the burden of proof was with them.

My response was to ask *them* to prove there *was* a God.

Or just to ignore them because I knew they couldn't.

Now that I'm a Christian, I can't prove God exists either. I can give you evidence of the reality of God, mostly the testimony of my own experience.[iv] But neither will I ask an unChristian to prove there's no God. It's a setup question. It does nothing to advance conversation and empathetic relationship, the things I'm really interested in when I'm talking with someone who believes differently than I do.

But relationship was not the goal of Christians who **accused me of being hypocritical because I celebrated Christmas**.

I guess it was an attempt to defuse my usual categorization of Christians as a bunch of hypocrites. "I know you are, but what am I?"

But recrimination doesn't usually (if ever) lead to relationship.

"Don't you know it's Jesus' birthday?" they'd ask. "If you don't believe in Jesus, how can you go to his party?"

My answer: I like presents.

An equally repulsive – in both senses of the word, odious and repellent – query was, "So why do you celebrate Thanksgiving? Who do you thank?"

My answer: I like turkey. I thank whomever cooks and carves it.

---

iv. Hey, that would make a great book!

Seriously, as a state employee for seven years during my unChristian era, I loved me some holidays! Thanksgiving and Christmas ceased being religious long, long ago. They are societal fixtures on the common calendar of our culture. That I celebrated Thanksgiving and Christmas along with the other several hundred million of my compatriots made me not a hypocrite but rather an American.

Christians, don't be a Grinch. Please don't do any of the other things in this chapter, but especially don't do that.

The only way some Christians could make sense of an unChristian like me was to assume I was mad at God up in heaven. So they would ask me, **"Why are you so angry at God?"**

If you're with me so far, you probably know how I answered this one. "If there's no God, there's no one to be angry at."

This question was a complete non-sequitur, a trap similar to "When are you going to stop beating your wife?"[v] Any kind of answer would be met with, "Ah ha! So you must believe in God if you're angry at Him!"

The thing is, I was angry about many things. My dad's suffering and death. Injustice. Hunger. Poverty. The Braves making the playoffs every year but not winning the World Series.

If those Christians who accused me of anger at God had given me a chance to express my resentment and disappointment rather than trying to trap me into admitting something I didn't believe, then perhaps we could have talked. Perhaps if they had listened to me – I mean really listened without thinking about what they would say next to advance their agenda – then maybe, just maybe, I would have listened to them.

But they were too busy following the script they learned in church or Sunday School or wherever. Inevitably if I tolerated the sales pitch long enough we'd get to **Hitler**.

Godwin's Law[vi] says that if an online discussion goes on long enough, Hitler will inevitably be invoked.

The same is true in evangelism.

"You know, Hitler/Stalin/Mao was an atheist. And look how

---

v. "When are you going to stop beating your wife?" is the classic trap question. Any response that answers the question is an admission.

vi. Not only did online pioneer Mike Godwin posit his famous law way back in 1990, he also adapted the mimetic concept of the meme to the world of online communication.

many millions he killed."

You didn't want to get into a debate with me about who has caused more misery in history, atheists or Christians.

You still don't.

Trust me on this. It's another great way to make sure Jesus never comes up in the conversation. Now we're talking about the Crusades and Columbus and Jim Jones and Pedophile Priests.

After I made it clear I had no interest in buying what they were selling, some exasperated evangelists would abandon their pitch with a parting shot absolutely guaranteed to elicit laughter and stifle meaningful conversation. It was delivered with great and pious sincerity, although it came across as passive aggressive:

"Well, God believes in *you*."

I'll just leave that little Hallmarkian phrase there without comment, and move on.

23

I Object!
(Amazing Grace 3)

I have heard all the objections to grace.

I have spoken some of them myself.

"It's too easy."

"It's not fair."

"Then just anybody can get in."

I hear those objections every time I preach or write about grace. It intrigues me that most of the folks who get offended are the ones who are already in church. Many Christians are truly threatened by the idea of God's extravagant grace. They're already in, after all.

Too many Christians are like the first home buyers in an exclusive, previously undeveloped area. They complain when all those "other people" start moving in.

"There goes the neighborhood."

Unspoken in our churches is this attitude: "We've got to keep out the undesirables."

Even more submersed is this: "They can come in when they're more like us."

Too many churches are really country clubs with a religious veneer. No wonder unChristians stay away!

Jesus wouldn't be welcomed into many of these Christian country club churches.

He hung out with undesirables like tax collectors and prostitutes.

He was a homeless wandering couch-surfer.

He challenged the political status quo.[i]

Jesus pronounced forgiveness before sins were confessed and before forgiveness was even requested.[ii]

We want to impose our broken human concept of forgiveness onto God. We don't want to forgive people who wrong us – or even just offend our country club sensibilities by listening to their music too loud or wearing their pants too low or whatever – until they've groveled and promised to be more like us.

God won't have it. God proclaims and exclaims grace through the cross.

Jesus died on that cross *while we were still sinners.*[iii] He didn't wait for us to get cleaned up. He cleans us up.

Good Christian folks are scandalized by grace. So we add conditions to God's gift.

When I was an unChristian, all I heard about from most Christians were the ifs:

God won't forgive you if. . .

God won't love you if. . .

There were very few Christians who said anything about grace. They told me about an angry God who was going to send me to hell unless I got *myself* straightened out and turned around. They talked a lot about my sin. They talked a lot more about other people's sin.

They did say Jesus on the cross had rescued me, but there was stuff I had to do.

Repent. (Whatever that meant.)

Get right with Jesus. (Even more baffling.)

Stop sinning, especially fornication, drinking, and, depending on whom you were talking to, dancing, playing cards, and listening to rock and roll.

---

i. Sometimes when I'm criticized for calling out government injustice or advocating for those on the margins, folks say I'm being "too political," as if our faith should not inform our involvement in the society in which we live. Remember this: Jesus was ultimately put to death by the political, not religious, system of his time.

ii. See the story of the paralyzed guy brought to Jesus by his friends in Mark 2. The dude never speaks, much less asks for forgiveness. He's lowered on a stretcher through a hole in a roof by his friends. There's no indication the guy even wanted to be there. But Jesus forgave him . . . and healed him.

iii. Romans 5:8.

And cursing. The "Best Christian" in most workplaces is the man or woman who just can't abide you cursing around them.

Something's wrong with that picture.

I understood them to mean God would love me *if* I stopped having fun and started being more like Church People.

Unsurprisingly, this didn't inspire me to run on over to the church on Sunday mornings.

Here's what I know now:

What I do or don't do has nothing to do with whether God loves me, forgives me, or saves me. Jesus lived, died and rose again for my forgiveness and salvation because God already loved me.

I've said it before: God's love, forgiveness, and salvation are gifts.

The only "if" in a gift is between the *g* and the *t*.

Overseas

24

Two Pairs of Socks in Vienna (Seed Planter Dan)

I entered Duke Law School in August, 1984. I had a full scholarship and an unfocused desire to save the world through Law.

I withdrew from Duke Law School at the end of January, 1985. I left with most of my savings, and an unfocused idea that law was just a big game for lawyers to make money.

At least that's the noble rationale I've developed over the years for my decision to turn my back on a top ten law school (built on the ashes of billions of cigarettes)[i].

Closer to the truth is probably that a semester was long enough to find out I didn't want to be a lawyer.

Or maybe I just wasn't ready to be *anything* for the rest of my life.

Bullseye!

I didn't attend any classes after I returned to Duke following Christmas break. I hung around for a few weeks because I had tickets to Bruce Springsteen's *Born in the USA Tour*. Those tickets provided my one tangible law school achievement. I stood in line all of one cold December night outside the Greensboro Coliseum while my law school buddies were studying for finals.

The concert was as amazing as you've heard.

Bruuuuuce!

But what to do next?

Why not travel?

---

i. The Duke family made their money in tobacco.

In February 1985 I set out on a three month journey through Europe accompanied only by my backpack. The couple thousand dollars of unused law school savings paid for my airfare on People's Express, the first of the bargain basement airlines ($149 flights from Newark to London!) and a Eurail Pass. There was enough left over for lodging and food until my return date if I stayed in hostels and ate lots of bread.

I watched every penny, franc, drachma, pence, lira, and pfennig.[ii] So when an American named Dan I'd just met on a train from Salzburg to Vienna told me he knew of a place I could stay in Vienna for $5 a night, I paid attention.

Dan served as a missionary in Yugoslavia[iii]. He was on some kind of break in Austria. I had no idea he was a missionary or even a Christian when I met him. He did not immediately ask me why God should let me into His heaven or if I'd filled up my God-hole.

No. Dan asked normal questions any American would ask a compatriot overseas. Where are you from? How long have you been in Europe? What's the best place you've been? Where's the nearest McDonalds?

It was only after I followed him to the cheap place we were going to stay in Vienna that I got suspicious. "Hey! What is this?"

"A Bible college."

I thought about finding somewhere less, well, spiritual to stay in my *Let's Go: Europe*[iv] book. But finding affordable accommodation was the biggest hassle of wandering from city to city. Plus five bucks a night couldn't be beat, even at the fleabag pensions and hostels I'd been frequenting. So I just asked him about his connection to the place. "Why here?"

That's when Dan told me about his missionary endeavors.

---

ii. The Euro, the common currency of much of Europe, did not begin circulating until January 1, 2002.

iii. Yugoslavia no longer exists. The country broke up in the early 90's, with its final demise in 1992. If you ever get a trivia question that contains the words "Yugoslavia" and "Dictator," you should answer with confidence, "Tito." You're welcome.

iv. What an awesome resource for anyone backpacking in Europe! And here's a handy tip at no extra charge – the book is huge so as you go tear out the pages of countries you have visited or don't plan to visit. That saves a lot of weight in your backpack. Of course these days backpackers probably don't take the physical book but rather have it on their phones or Kindles. Get off my lawn!

I braced myself for the inevitable conversion pressure but figured I could endure it for a couple of days.

Only the sales pitch never came. Not from Dan, anyway.

On the second night the president of the college invited us for dinner. When he found out I wasn't a Christian I thought he was going to throw us both out. But his shock over a heathen staying at his college gave way to the anticipation of winning a soul for Jesus.

It was like eating dinner at a rescue mission. You'll get fed, but you're going to get a sermon and an altar call first.

As the president employed some of the ineffective techniques described in a previous chapter, Dan did his best to redirect.

It turned out Dan was not theologically affiliated with the college. It was just somewhere he stayed on breaks from missionarying.

The president hammered away at doctrinal purity (the purity of *his* doctrine, anyway). But Dan's approach focused more on the cross than on right behavior. I was intrigued. It was the first time I heard a grace-based theology so clearly contrasted with salvation by doing the right stuff.

We finally escaped. The meal was good, but food is never as tasty when it's served with an agenda.

I had a blast the next couple days touring Vienna with Dan. Among lots of sightseeing, I saw my first opera at the world-famous Staatsoper. We got "standing places" tickets for seventy-five cents each, and met a guy in line who was studying music in Vienna on a Fulbright Scholarship. When the doors opened, the musician told us to "Follow me!" and we did. He showed us the best standing places as young people sprinted for them.

We ended up next to a railing at the front of the second balcony. People who knew the drill tied scarves to the railing to preserve the standing places. Neither Dan nor I had a scarf so I took off my extra pair of wool socks and tied them on instead. Our guide said he'd never seen that before, but the socks worked to hold our places while we explored the opera house before the show began.

I learned a lot from the Fulbright guy. Everything I knew about opera before that night came from Dick Motta[v]. So it was *all* new.

v. Dick Motta was coach of the Washington Bullets when he popularized the phrase, "The opera ain't over 'til the fat lady sings" during the 1978 NBA playoffs.

The particular opera that evening was *Faust* by Gounod. He told us it wasn't a "normal" production since the director was Ken Russell.

That was a name I knew. Russell directed the very strange movie version of The Who's *Tommy*.[vi] The opera was similarly weirdly wonderful featuring a giant skull with slot-machine eyes among other amazements.

After the opera Dan and I went to dinner with the Fulbright guy and some of his musician friends. Dan seemed as delighted to be learning new stuff as I was. To my greater surprise, he didn't seem offended or afraid of the obviously gay folks who joined us at the table.

It was a very different meal than the one hosted by the Christian college president, but Dan was just as comfortable.

I had a great adventure with Dan in Vienna. After touring Britain, the Netherlands, and Germany on my own, even an introvert like me appreciated having someone with whom to experience new things.

We discussed everything *but* Jesus, except when I initiated a theological conversation about what he did in Yugoslavia. That led to inquiries about *why* he did it.

Here's what I wrote in the journal I kept during that trip:

> *It was good traveling with someone for a few days for a change, and Dan was a good companion. He never tried to push his beliefs on me as some people of his persuasion might.*

Having walked away from faith and out of the church, I was looking for reasons to shut the door behind me permanently. There were plenty of Christians who gave me those reasons. But there were some like Dan who I believe God used to keep the door cracked open.

Why would God do that?

Because on June 21, 1963, God made a promise of persistence.

As I wrote back in Chapter Five, we Lutherans believe God actually does stuff in baptism. Baptism is not just an "outward sign of an inward change" that those who practice believer's baptism talk about. We believe baptism is a "means of grace," a conduit through which

---

vi. If anybody ever asks you to name the greatest rock band of all time, the correct answer is The Who.

God pours out grace.[vii]

God claimed me as God's child back in 1963, and promised never to let go. Nothing I could do would cause God to disown me or stop loving me – even denying God's existence. God would never stop reminding me what I had purposely forgotten.

That's what God did for me through people like Dan.

One more thing: at some point in our conversations Dan suggested if I ever wanted to find out more about being a Christian, I should read *Mere Christianity* by C. S. Lewis. When I started back toward faith almost ten years later, I remembered his advice.

Besides the Bible, *Mere Christianity* was the most influential book I read on my journey back to God.

So Christians . . . You never really know the impact you might have on someone else. The important thing is to be open to being a seed planter, without worrying about the harvest. After all, as Paul writes in 1 Corinthians 3, it is God who makes the seeds grow, not us.

The seeds Dan (and others) planted had to overcome stones implanted in the soil by overzealous proselytizers like the college president, but they gradually germinated into a renewed relationship with God.

---

vii. God's Word (both the Bible and Jesus) and Holy Communion are the other means of grace.

25

Magical Thinking with an Amen?

For the most part I was comfortable being an unChristian.

Except on airplanes.

On airplanes I strove to be a believer. A believer in heavier-than-air flight.

I could not convince myself that those huge jets could actually fly through the air. Filled with people and luggage and fuel and instrumentation and bags of peanuts, I knew the law of gravity would ultimately insist on a plunge.

There are bars in airports for people like I used to be.[i] Bars that open at dawn and don't stop serving alcohol until the final plane has left the tarmac.

To get to Europe I had to board one of those planes. To afford to get to Europe I had to book a bargain-basement flight which only added to my apprehension.

It was my first trip overseas.

Think about that word for a moment. Over-seas. On the over-night flight over-seas, if anything went wrong, we'd be under-water.

As the (hopefully) London-bound plane backed away from the Newark Airport gate, I tried to muster up the assurance that this 747 – this huge, heavy airplane – could actually achieve and sustain flight for eight hours.

---

i. I mean I am no longer a fearful flyer, not that I gave up alcoholic beverages. God led me to a denomination rooted in the theology of a German beer drinker – and beer maker. God knew what God was doing.

Yeah, right.

On this particular flight lurked a bigger doubter than me. For as we pulled away from the gate and began that big turn from backing out to moving forward – the big turn toward no-turning-back – the Voice of Doubt arose from the cheap seats just behind me.

"It's going to crash." The voice of this fellow-skeptic was not anywhere near as matter of fact as this simple statement appears on the page. But it wasn't full-throated terror, either. Somewhere between fact and terror was . . . assurance. Assurance of catastrophe. His was the proverbial Voice of Doom, reporting a terrible truth with only a tremor in his voice.

He said it again. "It's going to crash."

As for my nervousness about this flight to London?

This wasn't helping.

A flight attendant rushed to the man's row. "Sir, you'll have to be quiet."

But how do you shut up when you know what you have to say is the anti-gospel Truth?

"We have to turn around. It's going to crash."

Many passengers murmured their annoyance at the prophet. A man a row over tried reassurance. "Come on, let's get going and we'll be all right." Was this comforter sure, or was he trying to manage his own doubts?

Another voice made a more practical suggestion. "Somebody buy that guy a drink."

There was a titter of nervous laughter. It didn't affect the oracle at all. "I know this plane is going to crash. Please turn around. At least let me off."

The flight attendant walked to a phone that I guess called up to the pilot. Or maybe it went straight to God.

On a plane there's not much difference.

The plane came to a stop. They weren't going to mess around.

In a moment we were turning around.

They actually *believed* this guy? We were going back to the gate?

Good. Maybe I could take a train to London.

We got to the gate, the walkway was reconnected, and it was strongly suggested to the "It's going to crash" fellow that he find another way to England. All I saw was his gray suit as he swished up the aisle and was escorted off the plane.

They didn't believe him at all. He was just an apostate in their eyes. Planes don't crash. Everybody knows that.

Planes fly. And if you don't believe, then get lost; we don't want you around, because you might cause us to doubt. And what would happen then? People won't fly any more. They'll take the train, or the boat, or a car. Or they'll stay home. Then what happens to the airlines? What happens to the economy? No, *civilization as we know it* depends on our ability to get from Boise to Burlington in a few hours.

This is why churches have never done a great job of dealing with doubt. The Powers that Be fear the whole thing will fall apart if it's acknowledged as a normal and inevitable part of faith. But that's silly. As a church we should confront doubt as a community, not leave it to individuals to deal with and be tortured by it. If we talk about doubt, if we bring it into the open and admit its reality, then it loses its power over us.

You know what was crazy about the whole situation on the airplane? They wouldn't give anyone else a chance to follow the Chicken Little dude. Just get him off the plane, shut the thing back up, and once again we're backing toward London.

I wanted to get off. I really did. But did I have the guts to stand up in front of the, well, however many hundreds of people a 747 holds[ii] and say "I want to get off, too"? No way.

I stayed in my seat, but in my head I was imagining the interview with the survivor who'd just left the plane. The interview I'd never see because I didn't have the guts to follow him, the interview I'd never see because I'd be underwater or maybe washed up on some beach in Nova Scotia – an Unidentified Body speculated to be from the plane crash we told you about last week – and did you see the interview with the guy in the gray suit?

You've seen those interviews. After every plane crash, the news ghouls from ActionEyewitnessOnYourSideLiveLocalLatebreaking News find some guy – some crazy guy in a gray suit – Mr. "I was supposed to be on that flight but something told me/traffic was just

_____

ii. *Jeopardy!* wouldn't ask so I don't know.

worse that day/my wife had a feeling/my dog looked at me funny" – and interview him.

And we think, "Coincidence or . . ." and then the TV is showing the carnage and wreckage and smoke and always the investigators measuring something or standing around drinking coffee (I imagine them getting to the crash site and barking, "Black! And keep it coming!") and we've forgotten about the guy who was supposed to be on the flight and we start thinking about . . . who?

The people on the doomed flight? (It's always the "Doomed Flight" on the News, with that graphic of the cartoon plane spiraling down out of control on the screen behind the interracial Ken and Barbie anchorpeople).

Are we thinking about the former people who are now squashed charcoal? Of course not! We start thinking about ourselves and the next time we've got to fly and what the pilot said at the end of our last flight about, "Good luck on the most dangerous part of your flight, the drive home from the airport" – tell *that* to the folks on the Doomed Flight – and we wonder if it's worth the risk.

But, eventually, we line up again. I'd say, "Like lemmings," but really, what an overused metaphor (and according to Wikipedia lemmings really aren't suicidal). We get in the metal birds and take off, hoping our faith in aerodynamics will be rewarded with an uneventful flight – and maybe a headset that works on both channels so we don't just hear drums and backing vocals when they play the early Beatles' stuff recorded in those diametrically split tracks.

Speaking of music on airplanes, back when I was an unChristian I always took my Walkman when I flew and always listened to The Police: *Greatest Hits* when we took off. There really wasn't anything particularly reassuring about the music itself.

"De Do Do Do, De Da Da Da" is a great name for a song as well as excellent lyrics, but they don't exactly engender faith in flying.

The reason I needed to listen to Sting and the boys during takeoff is that I happened to have the tape in the Walkman for one flight, and we didn't crash, so . . . Why change what works? Like ballplayers who wear the same socks each day – without washing them – when they're on a hitting streak.

That's what's called "Magical Thinking." Have you ever had a friend who watched their favorite football team in THE SAME CHAIR each week eating THE SAME SNACKS wearing the SAME LUCKY SWEATSHIRT (and probably underwear)?

I have known such a friend.

Magical Thinking.

I used to think all Christians were Magical Thinkers. From the outside looking in, the ritual of a traditional worship service can look like an attempt to appease an angry God by doing things just the right way. On the very rare occasions I was in church during that time, the sameness of the services really bothered me. Now is when we stand up . . . sit down . . . stand up . . . let's all say the Lord's Prayer together . . . greet your neighbor . . . swing your partner do-si-do.

Yes, I added that last one.

But you get the idea. To the UnChristian, what we do in church may look like it's based on Magical Thinking. Especially the prayers.

If we say it just right then God will give us what we want.

Right?

Now that I'm on the inside, I know that's not what prayer is meant to be at all.

Prayer is pouring out our hearts to God.

In the book of Romans, we're promised the Holy Spirit will guide our prayers and will give us the words when we pray. Not only that, the Holy Spirit will intercede for us with groans – yeah, it says "groans" – when what we need to pray for is beyond words.

Praying is not rubbing the genie lamp or sitting on Santa's lap. To pray is to connect with God in heart, mind, and soul.

God promises to answer all of our prayers, but sometimes (often) God's answer is not a present but rather God's presence. Prayer allows us to experience God's promise that we never face anything on our own.

Praying with another person, or group of people, is to connect not just with God but with others.

We Christians don't do a good job of explaining this to folks outside the church. So it's no wonder prayer looks like superstition – like magical thinking.

One of the biggest problems, I think, is when we tell unChristians, "I'll pray for you."

Even if we do remember to pray for someone, when we make that promise then wait until our "prayer time" – or worse, wait until we get to church – we lose the opportunity to show someone what it means to connect with God and, more importantly, the chance to connect with another person.

One of the best pieces of advice I got, not as a pastor but as a new Christian, was never to say, "I'll pray for you."

Rather ask, "Can we pray together?"[iii]

That didn't happen too much when I wasn't a Christian.

I got lots of "I'll pray for you."

It felt like a dismissive pat on the head.

It's no wonder that the rare spiritual connections I experienced as an unChristian were most likely to occur with adherents of religions other than Christianity.

---

iii. Thank you, Karen!

26

Meeting Swamiji in India

The six of us bounced along in the blue-green van that apparently had no shocks. We twisted around the dusty roads snaking through the rocky hills outside Tumkur, India. A Beatles song played on the cassette player. The bobbing plastic figurines of Hindu deities on the dashboard seemed to bebop to the beat. We weren't sure where we were going, but our hosts said you couldn't be so close to Swamiji and not take advantage of the opportunity.

In 1993, I was chosen by local Rotary Clubs to spend a month in and around Bangalore, India, with five other "outstanding young adults"[i] on a Group Study Exchange[ii]. The nearby town of Tumkur was one of our excursions. While we were there we had the chance to visit the Sree Siddaganga Mutt run by Dr. Sree Sree Shivakumara Swamiji.

The Mutt is a spiritual center with a boys' residential and education institution outside Tumkur. At the time, it was home to over 5000(!) boys. The boys were all from rural families; 2000 were orphans. No one was turned away, regardless of caste or finances. They were provided with a place to live and with education from primary to post-doctorate(!!). The president of one of the Tumkur Rotary Clubs, we were told, is an attorney who grew up there, as did our exchange coordinator in Bangalore.

---

i. Surely there must have been a mistake!

ii. The Rotary Group Study Exchange sends non-Rotarian young adults on cultural and vocational exchanges, all expenses paid, to many parts of the world.

As we entered the grounds, I was amazed by the apparent harmony. Groups of boys walked along the road, played cricket, or just conversed in groups. When we got to the central complex of buildings and left the van, they eyed us with curiosity but none of the young men did anything to attract our attention. The boys all looked healthy and happy.

At the time I worked as a Juvenile Probation Officer for the Maryland Department of Juvenile Justice. I couldn't imagine DJJ or any private provider operating a facility for even 500 boys . . . but 5000?

We were shown into what must have been an administrative building about the size of a moderate ranch house. After removing our shoes, we were taken inside a cluttered office and invited to sit. Shortly, an elderly gentleman entered followed by a few other folks who must have worked there. At first we thought the older man must be Swamiji, but it turned out he wasn't elderly enough.

He told us that Swamiji was eighty-five and had been a holy man for sixty years. He only slept four hours a night. He spoke of Swamiji in reverent, awed tones that heightened my anticipation of meeting him.

The man also told us the place was supported entirely by donations.

"Here comes the pitch," I thought.

But then he added that because of the success of the former residents, they were financially very sound.

The man suddenly stopped speaking. There was a rustling as the people who worked at the place all stood up. So did we.

Swamiji slowly entered wearing a saffron robe. He looked every day of his eighty-five years, heavy-lidded like someone who did indeed sleep only four hours a night. But he smiled at us, and sat down at his letter-strewn desk.

Swamiji did not say much. But the words he practically mumbled in heavily accented English were compelling. He spoke about the necessity of doing away with the caste system and the discrimination it fostered. He sounded like a leader from the American Civil Rights movement.

Swamiji talked about how critical it was that every boy be made to feel at home and important. He answered a couple of questions. Mine was, "What is the most important thing done here?"

His answer: Education.

There was *something* compelling about Swamiji. An aura of serenity and wisdom enveloped him. We were with him for less than a half hour, but his presence lingered much longer.

I was of course skeptical that his affect was actually spiritual, but I was touched deeply by our audience with him. I left the Mutt still an agnostic at best. During my month in India I learned as much as I could about Hinduism. Even though I found much to respect about the religion, I affirmed that I was no Hindu.

But that brief time with Swamiji helped open me to the idea that there was some goodness, some binding force, some *thing* beyond the temporal I had yet to discover.

Did God use my encounter with this unChristian holy man to pull me closer?

Was Swamiji a seed-planter?

It wasn't long before the hosts who brought us said it was time to go. Swamiji gave us each an apple and we were out the door.

As we left the building, we stepped into a sea of children. The boys were gathering on the streets to go to evening prayers. There was a stage at the end of the street where we were told Swamiji would lead the service. Many of the boys crowded around the door and a few reached out their hands.

Being a cynical American who had encountered many beggars in India, I assumed they were asking for something. But then I noticed they held their hands with palms to the side, not up.

They just wanted to shake hands.

The trip to the van for my exchange group was sort of like being politicians after a campaign rally. Hundreds of smiling boys, most with foreheads marked with the Hindu Tilaka[iii], approached to have their hands shaken.

When we finally made it back to the van, they posed and grinned for pictures.

We were all touched by that place.

Who knows what they thought of us?[iv]

---

iii. Devotional markings, some just white and others colorful, painted with fragrant paste.

iv. According to its website, Sree Siddaganga Mutt is still going strong, but Swamiji died in 2019. He was 111 years, 295 days old.

Dad

27

I Want the Free One
(Amazing Grace 4)

One of my parishioners told me she once answered the phone and an excited voice said, "You have WON! You have won a FREE trip to Disney World!" The prize included airfare, hotel, food, and tickets to Disney.

Delighted but dubious, my church member responded, "That's great! How can I get this free trip?"

The telemarketer replied, "Well, what you have to do to get started on your FREE trip is to give me your credit card number. There's just a $250 processing fee."

My parishioner hung up.

Was that really a free trip?

I received one of those overgrown junk mail postcards a while back. It invited my family and me down to Colonial Williamsburg for three days and two nights. All expenses paid! It was a gift from the company who mailed it. They would put us up in a nice place, feed us, and even give us tickets to the historic area and to the Busch Gardens theme park.

That sounded great!

I called the 800 number on the mailing.

The smooth gentleman who answered said, "Yes! The trip is absolutely free. It is our gift to you and your family. All you have to do is agree to attend a brief presentation about our valuable timeshare property. Just experience this exciting presentation to get your free trip."

I didn't go.

Was that a free trip?

I remember going grocery shopping with my dad when I was growing up. Equipped with a list from my mom, he did all the shopping at Safeway. One thing he hated at the store was Buy One, Get One Free specials.

We'd be in the detergent aisle and there'd be a big, colorful BOGOF sign under the big boxes of Tide.

My dad would always say, "I want the free one."

And I, being an argumentative brat, would always bait him. "You have to buy one to get the free one."

"Then it's not free."

He was right.

If you have to pay anything or do anything or buy anything, it's not free. It's not a gift. It's not grace.

————

Time for another Paul story!

It's told in the sixteenth chapter of the Bible book of Acts. After his conversion, Paul traveled throughout the Roman Empire telling people about Jesus. He moved around a lot because he was called to spread the Word, but also because his message pissed people off and he kept getting beaten or thrown into jail or a Daily Double of both.

In Acts 16, Paul and his traveling partner Silas are in a northeastern Greek town called Philippi. As usual, Paul's gotten himself into trouble. Why he's in trouble is a good story about a slave girl who can tell the future and her angry owners, but it's too involved to tell here.

To make the long story short, the girl's owners have Paul and Silas arrested, stripped, beaten, and tossed into jail, which typically was little more than a subterranean pit. The jailer is given strict instructions to keep an eye on them.

He throws Paul and Silas into the deepest, darkest, most isolated part of the jail, then puts them in stocks so they cannot move.

So what do Paul and Silas do?

They pray and sing praises to God.

Luke, who wrote Acts in addition to the Gospel that bears his name, tells us the other prisoners listened to the praying and singing. He doesn't tell us whether they were inspired by the worship or aggravated because they couldn't get to sleep.

About midnight, the earth rocks and rolls. The seismic vibrations cause the doors to fly open, and the prisoners' chains to fall off.

The tremor jolts the jailer awake. To his despair, he sees the open doors and figures all the prisoners under his watch escaped. Distraught at the capital consequences of allowing especially Paul and Silas to slip away, he decides to end it all. He is just about to off himself when a voice comes from deep inside the prison.

"Stop! We're still here! We didn't leave! It's Paul!"

The jailer is impressed. He wonders how he can get what Paul and Silas have, singing and praying all night in the direst circumstances, and not fleeing when they got the chance.

How can he get that kind of freedom? How do you get the kind of freedom that doesn't require you to walk out an open prison door in order to be free?

How can that happen in my life?

The jailer condensed all those questions into a single query:

"What must I do to be saved?"

But that is the wrong question. It is like these wrong questions I have collected over the years:

> *An airplane crashes on the border between France and Switzerland. Where do you bury the survivors?*[i]

> *An electric train is traveling north at seventy miles per hour. The wind is from the west at fifteen miles per hour. Which direction is the smoke blowing?*[ii]

> *How many of each animal did Moses take on the ark?*[iii]

The jailer's question is like those. "What must I do to be saved?" There is no right answer because the question is flawed.

There is nothing you have to do to be saved.

---

i. You don't bury survivors.

ii. Electric trains don't blow smoke.

iii. None. That was Noah.

There is nothing you can do to be saved.
It's all been done.

Paul's answer to the jailer reflects this reality. He says, "Believe in the Lord Jesus and you will be saved, you and your household."

Believe in Jesus and what Jesus has already done for you. There is nothing else you need to do.

And belief is not something you and I do; it is something God creates in us. Faith is a gift.

It's grace.

I most certainly did not understand any of that when I was an un-Christian. Perhaps if more Christians made it clear, more seeds would have been planted.

But many Christians don't understand it, either. They are working hard so God will forgive them, so God will save them . . . so God will love them.

Sometimes I have trouble wrapping my head around it.

God's love, forgiveness, and salvation really are free.

But they cost Jesus everything.

28

Stuck!

My dad's car was a hulking, white Ford LTD. It maneuvered like an aircraft carrier. Next to other cars, it was like a modern middle linebacker, a monstrous combination of size, power, and speed.

I had to be careful with my dad's LTD because for him cars were Tools Not Toys.

Like many suburban middle-class adolescents, my driver's license opened a new world of dating possibilities. That first license was soon followed by my first real girlfriend. One night we were out and decided we needed some time alone.

You know, to talk.

But this is not that kind of story.

We drove around awhile and I noticed a dirt road going back into some woods. I decided a car as big and powerful as mine would work fine off-road.

My brain was not the organ with which I was thinking.

I turned the LTD down the dirt road, which turned out to be more of a sandy horse trail. If you've ever spent much time in Florida, you know it rains intensely many afternoons about 3:30. This was one of those days, so it was a *wet and muddy* sandy horse trail.

You may see where this is going.

Or not going.

We were just out of sight of the main road when I noticed the tires started spinning faster than we were moving. No problem – I just pushed the accelerator harder and let that big ol' engine do its thing.

But the resistance only got worse.

Maybe this trail wasn't such a good idea after all.

I threw the car into reverse.

The behemoth wouldn't budge. The back tires had settled into a muddy dip and weren't climbing out. I vaguely remembered a lesson in Driver's Ed about how to get a car moving that's stuck in the snow – a strange topic for Florida, I thought at the time. You were supposed to rock the car by shifting back and forth between reverse and drive until you were moving.

So we rocked.

But we didn't roll.

I opened the door and hopped out. My feet sank into the sandy mud. It brought memories of *Gilligan's Island* quicksand. Briefly I hoped it would pull me under like it did Gilligan (leaving only his sailor hat) and solve my problem.

At least it would no longer be my problem.

I barked at my girlfriend to slide over in the driver's seat. I sprinted to the back of the car and dug into the muck as best I could. If we could just move the back tires out of that gully, we could get some momentum going and back out. I put my shoulder against the fat ass of the car.

I hollered at my girlfriend to put 'er in drive and gun the engine.

The wheels spun and I got a gritty shower.

Mud and sand pelted me until I yelled, "STOP!" She took her foot off the accelerator less than immediately and I let her know I was extremely disappointed in her slow reaction time.

I was less than gallant under pressure.

Panicked, I started digging around the tires with my hands. It was my dad's car. His transportation to work. My dad was big on taking care of things, making them last. "Always return something in better shape than you took it."

I had to get that car out of there . . . or else.

After several minutes of fruitless pawing at the mud, I stood up, exhausted.

I thought I remembered a phone booth[i] not too far up the main

---

i. No cell phones in 1979, unfortunately. Hypothetical younger readers, back then pay phones, sometimes in glass booths, were fairly common.

road.

My girlfriend and I began a march of shame.

Now, I wasn't an admitted atheist or even agnostic yet. But already I had lots of doubts about God and since I'd been in high school I didn't even need to volunteer anywhere on Sundays to get out of going to church.

On that walk, though, I offered God a variety of deals:

Get Dad's car out and I'll go to church.

Get Dad's car out and I'll read the Bible.

Get Dad's car out and I'll never go "offroad" with my girlfriend again.

Get Dad's car out and we'll even – this killed me but I meant it at the time – give up our "homework" at her house after school before her parents got home.

Apparently none of those offers were sufficient for God to take the deal.

We reached the phone booth. I had four dimes. I started by calling my three closest friends. I'm not sure what I thought they could do, but it didn't matter because it was Friday night and three out of three weren't home.

I had one dime left.

And one more prayer. I prayed it as I dialed the digits of my home phone number.

"God, please let my mom answer the phone."

"Hello," my dad said.

Power of prayer, my ass.

For a moment, I considered telling my dad I'd lost the car. "Don't know what happened to it. One minute it was there . . ."

But I knew he wouldn't buy it. So I told him it was stuck.

He said he'd be there as soon as he could.

When he got there, he didn't say anything but it was clear from his clipped speech and clenched jaw he was pissed. I was in the worst trouble of my life. I'd gotten my father's car stuck. And what was I doing driving down that dirt road in the first place? I don't think he bought my, "We were looking for a place where we could talk alone because we never get time just by ourselves" any more than you did.

He saw the car wasn't going to budge. We walked back to the pay phone. He called a tow truck.

Then came a loooong, silent wait.

Eventually, the tow truck got there and pulled the car out. I watched my father pay the driver. Every bill he counted into the driver's hand felt like a slap upside my head. My dad hadn't spanked me in years and I didn't think he'd start again now, but it was like he was counting out the days, months . . . years of my impending groundation.

I was sure my driving days were done.

After the tow truck pulled away, Dad said in a quiet, flat voice, "Take your girlfriend home, then . . . Come. Straight. Home."

I didn't talk to my girlfriend at all on that drive. Fear will silence you that way.

When I got home, I sat in the car for a while, saying goodbye. After all, it was probably the last time I'd be able to drive, at least until I got out of college and moved out on my own. When I finally got out, I took my time examining the car. I really looked at the formerly white, now muddy gray, LTD for the first time. It was a mess, inside and out.

I was in no hurry to get inside the house.

Finally, I went in. There was my father in his La-Z-Boy recliner.

Except he wasn't reclining.

There was no point in excuses or explanations. "Dad, I'm really, really . . . really sorry."

He kind of glanced at me before he spoke. I knew I'd never drive again but I had a moment to wonder what other punishments were coming. Grounding? Extra chores?

The rack?

Slowly, Dad rose from his chair. He looked right at me. "I know you're sorry. Just get the car cleaned up. I'm going to bed." And down the hall he went.

That was it. I thought he was going to let me have it the next morning, but he didn't say anything about it. My dad died not too many years later when I was twenty-five, and he never said another word about that night.

I was simply . . . forgiven.

My dad taught me more about grace in that moment than I learned in years of being forced to go to church and Sunday School.

But it was also because of my dad that I would reach the apogee[ii] of my separation from God.

---

ii. I struggle to remember "apogee" is the farthest point in the moon's orbit around the earth and "perigee" is the closest. Maybe you can do better. You may have heard of a Super Moon, the full moon that happens when the moon is close to its perigee. What is the full moon called that happens at the apogee? A Micro Moon. Now you know.

29

Too Smart for Dad

William Stanley Simpson, always known as "Stan" except to his mother-in-law who called him "Stanley," grew up in the 1940s. His widowed father with three kids married a widowed mother with three kids and that's the way they became the Simpson bunch.[i]

My dad's dad was a milkman who could only afford to send his oldest son to college. Dad was not the oldest, but he took night classes and got an associate's degree in accounting. His dream had been to serve in the Navy – he was big into the Sea Scouts as a teenager – but a diagnosis of juvenile diabetes when he was seventeen put an end to that.

It was the first of the health issues that would eventually put an end to everything way too soon.

Instead of the Navy he went to work for his second love, the railroad. He started out with Seaboard Air Line Railroad in his hometown of Norfolk, Virginia. Soon after he married my mom, his high school sweetheart, he moved to Richmond where the newly merged Seaboard Coastline Railroad was headquartered.

It is fitting to start with family when talking about my dad. There was nothing more important. All the games when I sat on the bench in Little League – he was there. He loved to watch football on television, especially his beloved Bears, but Sunday afternoons were family time. Dad gave up many opportunities to sit in his La-Z-Boy in front of the color console TV so he could go on picnics and walks in the

---

i. Younger readers may not know "the Simpson bunch" is a reference to the end of the Brady Bunch theme song.

park and country drives with us.

Yes, he had a temper. He was old-fashioned and administered the occasional spanking with his hand or belt when I was younger. But usually his bark was worse than his bite.

"No son of mine is going to have hair covering his ears."

And yet, when I grew my hair long in high school he never said a word.

When I got into high school he figured even with mom working he wasn't going to be able to afford to send two kids to college. So he got a second job.

I remember picking him up at Roto-Rooter, where he worked as a night dispatcher, when he got off at eleven. He looked exhausted and worn after another sixteen-hour day. I had to pick him up because he took the bus to the railroad office and then again to the second job so I could have the car to do whatever it was I did – soccer or tennis practice, dates, time with friends, working a couple nights a week. A few times I fell asleep waiting for the time to go pick him up and got there late. He grumbled a little but mostly he was glad I was okay.

I wish I'd appreciated him more. You see, not only did I decide I was too smart for God.

I decided I was too smart for my dad.

Mark Twain supposedly said, "When I was a boy of fourteen, my father was so ignorant I could hardly stand to have the old man around. But when I got to be twenty-one, I was astonished at how much the old man had learned in seven years." It took me way past twenty-one to be astonished at how much my father had "learned." I guess I was even more arrogant than Mark Twain.

Like most little kids I wanted to be like my dad; like many adolescents I wanted to be everything he wasn't.

Once I was a teenager, the emotion I mostly remember my father provoking in me was annoyance. He didn't understand how the modern world worked.

He didn't understand *anything* as well as I did.

My dad was not progressive on issues of race. When the *King* miniseries about Martin Luther King, Jr. was broadcast in 1978 when I was sixteen, I wasn't allowed to watch it on the "big TV." I was exiled to my room to view the life of "that troublemaker" on the twelve-inch black and white.

Dad told jokes around the dinner table that poked fun at all kinds of ethnic groups, and LGBTQ folks as well.

They were mostly silly. I'm sure he would say harmless, but definitely demeaning to those who were the butt of the joke.

He was a product of his times, growing up in the segregated south of the 40s and 50s. And I hated that about him, his narrow-minded view of the world, his conservative republican politics, his old-fashioned religion.

His world seemed so small, and I wanted to take on the whole world. I wanted to change the world, to change *his* world. And he didn't understand that.

He just loved me. But I couldn't see that for all the judgment I heaped upon him.

Then he got sick.

It was the summer between my junior and senior year of high school. I was at my grandmother's in Virginia for my annual week of being spoiled beyond belief. My mom called and told me I needed to fly home. Dad was going into the hospital. He needed open-heart surgery – a triple bypass.

He was forty-two.

He didn't smoke or drink. Although he may have been a little overweight, he was far from obese. But all the eggs and red meat his diabetes doctors told him to eat caught up with him. That, and genetics.

The night before the surgery, our family gathered in Dad's hospital room. We talked and laughed. There was no way he was going to let us see him scared. We were interrupted by a nurse with a razor. "I know what you're going to do with that!" he said in mock horror. Back then, they shaved you from your neck to your toes for open-heart surgery. The doctor said the itching from the hair growing back would be almost as bad as the pain.

My sister and I gave my dad hugs, and we were out of there.

What bothered me most about the surgery was that they were going to stop his heart while they did the actual bypass. A machine would keep the blood pumping, but he would be *dead*, right? No heartbeat equaled death, as far as I knew.

The big surgical milestone would be when they got his heart started. I thought of it like trying to turn over a car engine on a cold morning. You turn the key and give it some gas.

And hope it roars to life.

The next day crawled as we waited out the hours of surgery. I don't remember if I prayed or not; I probably threw out some "just in case" prayers, which was pretty much the state of my relationship with God.

Finally, the doctor emerged. Everything had gone fine. My dad gave the doc a big grin when they told him the surgery was over. Everything was going to be all right.

But I was old enough to know *everything* was never all right.

Later, I got to see Dad briefly in the Cardiac Care Unit. Nothing prepared me for how he was going to look. The pillar of our family now seemed small and shriveled. He was as pale as the sheets. Machines clicked, pinged, and swished all around him. A smoky oxygen mask covered his mouth and nose, but you could see his teeth – or the startling lack of them. I had never seen my dad without the dentures that replaced his two front teeth. To see that void heightened my unease.

Someone dimmed the lights . . . I saw the needles piercing Dad's arm and one skewering his neck . . . and the lights got dimmer. Everyone started to fade away . . .

The next thing I knew someone had poured Windex into my nostrils and up into my brain.

So that's what smelling salts did.

From that day I began to wonder if my plan to become a doctor was a great idea for someone who passed out in hospitals. In fact, I would avoid hospitals and people in them for years. Too many sick people in there . . . too much death.

(That's another irony of God's plan for me to be a pastor: I am often in hospitals, nursing homes, and hospices. Like I often say, it's God's plan; it was never mine.)

It wasn't just seeing my dad like that. It was being so close to death, and death being so close to me. I had never been to a funeral, not even when my grandfather died. My parents never talked to me, or even in my presence, about his death. It was the same silence when neighbors died. Even when a kid in my middle school died by suicide, they never mentioned his death.

I'm sure they thought it was for our own good, but my parents tried to keep us in a protective cocoon by denying the reality of death. So I was never prepared for dealing with it in a healthy way.

Nor did I have the tools to deal with what happened next to my father.

The next day my mom rushed off to the hospital. There'd been a "setback."

Later I found out they got my dad to sit up . . . and he had a stroke. He was partially paralyzed and couldn't talk. The stroke doctor said he was better off than another patient that day who could talk but couldn't understand anything people said to him. "Can you imagine how frustrating *that* would be?"

Yeah, my dad sure was lucky.

But Dad was a fighter. They weren't sure he'd bounce back from the stroke, but he willed himself to talk again. Speech therapy was demeaning, like going back to kindergarten again, but he dove into it with determination.

At first he sounded like someone who had just moved here from a country where they didn't speak English; my mom said he sounded like the Tim Conway character, Mr. Tudball, on The Carol Burnett Show.[ii]

Dad was afraid he'd have to quit his part-time job at Roto Rooter because he needed to be understood when he dispatched trucks over the radio. But six weeks later, he was back at both jobs and all was back to normal.

His health challenges weren't over, though.

Three years later, Mom and Dad were shopping at the mall when he became violently ill. He was rushed to the hospital, where he had his appendix removed. It got infected. He ended up spending more time hospitalized for the appendix than he had for the bypass.

I visited him one afternoon. I think it was the pain medication, but for the first and only time he shared with me his awareness of mortali-

---

ii. You have to be at least as old as me to get that reference – look it up on YouTube if you aren't and don't. One of my favorite memories of my dad is him sitting in that La-Z-Boy watching CBS's Saturday night lineup of Mary Tyler Moore, Bob Newhart, and Carol Burnett. Sometimes he laughed so hard he cried. (Also, if they'd talked about things like "celebrity crushes" back in those days, his would have been Mary Tyler Moore, I bet.)

ty. "The doctor said if they didn't have antibiotics, I would have died." He paused. "I would have *died*."

Three years later, I was home for the summer from college. Dad went to the doctor for a pain in his back.

He found out it wasn't a pulled muscle.

It was cancer.

Multiple myeloma.

He was forty-eight.

30

Kicking Death's Ass

Dad endured chemotherapy that summer. It made him terribly sick. One afternoon, I came home from my summer job to sounds of Dad heaving his guts out in the bathroom. Strangled screams accompanied each bout of retching. Bending over the toilet sent spasms of pain through his back.

I had never heard anybody in so much pain.

I collapsed on my knees in front of our living room couch. "Make it stop. Make it stop!" I cried out to the God I denied existed, the God that Dad held onto with everything he had. "Make it stop and I'll do anything. What has he done to deserve this, you son of a bitch?! How can you be such a cruel bastard? What the hell did all his singing in the choir and being church treasurer and all that stuff for the church – for you – get him?

"Why are you torturing him?"

"Do you enjoy it?"

"You're not even there. The hell with you!"

Earlier, I referenced Romans chapter eight where Paul says the Holy Spirit helps us pray with groans too deep for humans to understand. I'm not sure if my pitiful, petulant cry was Holy Spirit inspired, but it was, in its way, a prayer.

These days I often say in funeral sermons, especially following "bad" deaths, that it is okay to get angry at God. God can take it. Anger keeps the relationship going until the emotion fades.

It would take a long time before my anger faded.

But Dad did get better.

He went into the hospital. He was there a long time before they got the nausea under control.

He continued to submit to the poisonous chemo even as it destroyed the nerves in his left leg. For the rest of his life, he had to walk with a cane. Somewhere he got an Irish shillelagh[i]. He was quite proud of it. He needed something to feel good about.

Unexpectedly, dad's cancer went into remission. As Richard Pryor once said about John Wayne, Dad had "kicked death's ass."

I was out in the world by then, but his illness brought us closer. The things that irritated me about him just weren't that important.

Too bad I didn't figure that out sooner. The clock was ticking.

---

i. A shillelagh is a hefty piece of wood used as a walking stick these days, but which were originally used in Ireland as cudgels for fighting, specifically dueling.

31

Two Phone Calls

Sunday, April 13, 1986

Forty-six year old Jack Nicklaus started the final round of the 1986 Masters four shots off the lead. There were lots of golfers between him and the leader, Greg Norman. Nicklaus had won more major tournaments than anyone,[i] but it had been six years since he'd won a major. No one expected him to contend, but Nicklaus was on fire that day. On the front nine, he shot a record-setting round that vaulted him improbably into the lead.

I watched in awe at my apartment in North Carolina. I rooted for the Golden Bear. Heck, I even had his autograph from a trip to the TPC Golf Tournament with Dad when I was in high school.

My dad didn't teach me to play golf, but he got me my first clubs and we played a few rounds before his leg gave out.

He was terrible.

He insisted on sinking every putt, no matter how close to the cup. There were no 'gimmies' for my dad. You didn't break or bend the rules, even if everybody else did. Even if there was golfing courtesy when you weren't playing in a tournament.

About halfway through Jack's historic back nine, my phone rang. It was dad.

"Are you watching this?"

"Yeah. It's amazing, isn't it?"

---

i. And he still has. Nicklaus won eighteen major championships: six Masters, five PGAs, four US Opens, and three British Opens.

We watched the rest of the Masters that afternoon "together." This was back when you paid for long distance by the minute, but my usually-frugal dad kept me on the phone until Nicklaus put on the green jacket.[ii]

There was something wondrous – now I would say "holy" – about that Sunday afternoon, sharing a sports miracle long distance when I was twenty-four and my dad was fifty. It took our relationship to the next level.

After that, I got home more often to spend more time with him. We took a trip together to see spring training baseball the next February, something we hadn't done for years. I couldn't believe how he climbed up to the top of the grandstand with one good leg and a cane. For the first time since I was a little kid who believed his dad could do anything, I believed my dad could do anything.

Monday, September 21, 1987

I remember the black phone.

I was teaching at a boarding school outside Atlanta. It was breakfast time. I was in the dining hall, eating with some students. One of the other faculty members emerged from the Teachers' Lounge.

"You have a phone call."

Was it something in his voice? Was it some sort of premonition? I shuddered.

The black phone sat on a table in a corner of the Teachers' Lounge. The receiver lay next to it. I picked it up. "Hello?"

Mom's voice, muffled and further away than the 350 miles to home. "Your father is gone."

Tears. I couldn't stop them. I managed to tell my mom I'd drive right home. I'd be there in six hours.

Six hours of tears. Driving. Shouting at God not because I believed God was there but because I needed an object for my fury. All that dad had gone through. He beat a bypass and a stroke. He fought off the appendix infection. And he wrestled cancer into remission.

In chapter 32 of Genesis, Jacob wrestles with an angel. He grapples all night even after his hip bone breaks. At the end of the fight, he is

----

ii. Champions of The Masters are presented with green jackets.

renamed Israel which means, *He wrestles with God.*

Like Jacob, my dad emerged from his fight with a limp, and more importantly with a new identity, at least in my eyes.

So all that got him . . . what?

Dying in his sleep in the middle of the night? Nobody got to say goodbye?

Well, fuck you, God. We're done. Over and out. Again.

Somewhere in the course of that ride I shifted from a sometimes squishy agnostic who might pray to God once in a while "just in case" to a confirmed atheist convinced the world was random, not guided by any higher power, certainly not by any loving God. If a good man like my father could suffer, and fight, only to die at fifty-two, then there was no justice or mercy. At least no *divine* justice or mercy.

We're on our own.

Look, I know people who have been through far worse than my dad. But I was already a skeptic, already cynical, already teetering on the edge of burying any remnant of my relationship with God. How could you have a relationship with someone who didn't exist? How could God tolerate war and hunger and Jim and Tammy Bakker? None of it made sense.

Nothing was supposed to make sense.

It was all random.

At the funeral home viewing in Jacksonville, I asked to be set up somewhere I didn't have to see Dad's body. I said I didn't want to remember him that way, but that was only partially true.

I didn't want to confront death, the Great Nothingness at the end of a pointless life.

As I stood there with my back to the casket, I watched the room overflow with people I'd never seen before. Many of them wanted to tell me what a good man my dad had been. They came with stories of times Stan helped them out at work or at church or whatever, times when he had a kind word or a bad joke that made them feel better. I didn't realize how beloved my dad was until that viewing. I was so proud of him.

But angrier. What did it get him? He wasn't around to hear the accolades.

We shipped his body to Norfolk. He was finally carried back to old

Virginia. No way was he going to be buried in Florida.

I wore sunglasses inside and out for four days in Norfolk. No one was going to see my bloodshot eyes. No one was going to know I'd been crying, especially since I'd been crying less for him – he was gone – than for myself.

The only person who got any emotion out of me was the pastor at my grandmother's church where the funeral service was going to be held.

"You didn't know my father. You're not going to talk about my father. Do what you have to do, but I'll do the personal stuff." I was a right asshole to the good old parson.

But he remained, well, pastoral. "You can talk about your father. Just give me a copy of what you're going to say so I can finish it for you if you can't get through it."

"I'll get through it," I said through gritted teeth. I was rude and condescending. After all he was an idiot who not only believed in God but worked for the non-entity, spreading false hope in return for all the cash he could shake out of people into the offering plate.

Yes, I understand that is some folks' perception of the job that is mine now. I just hope I am as compassionate, empathetic, and understanding as my grandmother's pastor was with me when I, in God's great ironic plan, am on the other side of such conversations.

The evening before the funeral, Dad's relatives gathered at my grandmother's house and shared memories of him. I stayed up all night compiling them into what I titled, "William Stanley Simpson: A Family Tribute."

I got through it.

Maryland

32

Love Stinks
(Seed Planter Doug)

Four years after my encounter with Dan in Vienna, I met Doug.

I started working at the Maryland Department of Juvenile Justice in 1989. I was actually hired because of Doug, or, more exactly, to help him. He was the only Juvenile Probation Officer in rural-but-becoming-suburban Queen Anne's County, just over the Chesapeake Bay Bridge from Annapolis and commutable from Baltimore and Washington. The department created my position as the county's second Probation Officer in response to Doug's workload.

From the time I started working with him, Doug was upfront about his faith. He kept a Bible on his desk, even though our supervisor had concerns.[i] When office talk centered on weekend activities, Doug's contribution usually recounted a church function of some sort.

Doug was too uptight and straight-laced for my taste, the only taste that really mattered in those days.

I tended to dismiss most of Doug's opinions because of his faith. I did not regard him as someone who thought for himself but rather, like most if not all Christians, as sort of a puppet whose ideas and imagination were controlled by an ancient book and fantastical God.

But.

---

i. Even now as a Christian I think his concerns were valid. We were supposed to conduct hearings and supervision impartially; so an unChristian young person or parent who saw the Bible might legitimately wonder if they were going to get a fair shake. Not that Doug himself was ever biased, as far as I know, but appearances matter in our justice system.

Doug never preached at me.

Very rarely did he even launch prayers in my direction. When he did, the situation was extraordinary, like when he left a note on my desk with a prayer for "Justice and Mercy" on the day I had to go to court about an accident I caused that totaled three cars. He knew I was nervous about the court appearance. I received the prayer as more empathetic than evangelistic.

I appreciated his efforts on my behalf, even if I considered them futile. It must have meant something to have stuck in my memory; twenty-some years later, I still remember thinking about his Justice and Mercy note: "More of the latter and less of the former, please."

There were two things Doug did to stealthily plant seeds of faith. By "stealthily" I mean neither I, nor he, had any idea those seeds were being sown.

First was his dedication to doing prison ministry. Every Thursday night on his own time he would enter the Eastern Pre-Release Center and do whatever he did with the inmates there. He didn't talk about the specifics much, but I knew it involved God somehow. I admired Doug being a Christian who actually listened to what Leader Jesus said. I knew somewhere in the Bible Jesus said it was pretty important to visit folks in jail.[ii] What I expected from Christians, especially fairly fundamentalist Christians like Doug, was nothing but judgment for those who had gotten themselves locked up.

It is ironic (or maybe not if you believe in a Divine Plan as I do now) that since 2009 one of my primary ministries outside the church I'm called to serve has been . . . prison ministry. Every third Friday of the month I go into the Maryland Correctional Institute at Jessup (MCIJ) to lead worship with a team of lay people.

Now I understand why this ministry was so important to Doug. It is an outreach of hope to people locked in negativity. It is a proclamation of freedom (in Christ) to folks who are in bondage - and not just physically. For some it is the only visit they receive from people outside. Those men worship with a hunger for the Gospel. When I talk about grace and God's unconditional, no-matter-who-you-are-no-matter-what-you've-done love, I am more likely to see tears than

---

ii. Now I know it was in Matthew 25:36: "I needed clothes and you clothed me, I was sick and you looked after me, I was in prison and you came to visit me."

the shrugs that often greet the proclamation of the Good News outside the prison walls.

Of course I knew none of this when I worked with Doug. I just thought his prison ministry was a nice thing he did. It was significant to me because I associated Christians with surface faux-niceness, not genuine acts of love and service.

Doug's second illustration of stealthy seed-planting was less formal but more sacrificial.

Our office was in Centreville, a town surrounded by rural farmland. Every day on his way to work Doug passed a house – more of a shack – where Edgar lived. Edgar was old. It was hard to say how old because it was clear he had been ridden hard and put away wet, as they say in the country. He'd lived a rough life.

When Edgar needed to get to town, he would stand out beside the country road in front of his house. He wouldn't extend his thumb or anything. He would just intently watch the cars approach at fifty or so miles per hour. He'd swivel his head as they whizzed by, then turn his attention back up the road. He would do this until one of those cars stopped to pick him up.

Not many did. Cars moved quickly past him because it was hard to tell he even needed a ride. The rare folks who picked him up only did it once. Edgar apparently observed an Elizabethan bathing schedule.[iii] Something of him more than memory lingered in the car long after he took that ride.

Doug was the exception.

I could always tell if Doug had picked up Edgar. The aroma trail began at the base of the stairs that led to our suite of offices and strengthened as I ascended. Our office professional would be waving one hand in front of her squinched up nose, while spraying the sickly sweet smell of air freshener with the other. Her efforts succeeded only in increasing its noxious complexity.

Doug's office was next to mine. On those days I would shut my door, but that was only partially successful. It might have helped to

---

iii. You may have heard the old saw that "Queen Elizabeth took a bath once a month, whether she needed it or not." Folks in the Middle Ages believed baths could actually be harmful, opening the pores to the ingress of a variety of disease-causing vapors. This belief is also common among pre-adolescent boys.

stuff wet towels under the door like they tell you to do in hotel fires, but I had no towels at hand.

I could only imagine what his car smelled like after Edgar-transport, but Doug seemed to be immune.

He had immunity by choice. It was more important for him to give Edgar a ride, to help him out when he needed it and no one else would, than to avoid the unfortunate result.

Doug didn't just bring Edgar to town. He would also walk with him to the various agencies he needed to visit, helping steer him through the opaque bureaucracies.

How sad, I thought.

Doug can't help himself because he has to do what he thinks God is telling him to do.

That was the easy way out for me. It kept me from considering that perhaps faith could have a positive impact on a person, and on those the person encounters.

But despite my dismissal, Doug's interactions with Edgar were indeed a seed. Seeds don't have to be spectacular, newsworthy gestures. The seeds from which mighty plants grow are tiny, as are the seeds from which my faith eventually sprouted.

Doug, Dan, and the other seed-planters you've met in this book were just doing what they believed Christians should do. They were doing their best to be Christ-like, to *be* Christ for those they encountered. It wasn't just their actions though. They made clear *why* they acted the way they did. They were clear about *who* motivated their actions.

To make an impact, they didn't need to be all up in my faith about the state of my eternal soul. If they had been, it would have had the opposite effect (see "How to Chase Away an UnChristian").

Just by living faithfully, they provided an alternative to my stereotypical picture of Christians.

They provided an alternative to being an UnChristian, an option I would not even begin to consider until years after Dan and Doug planted their seeds.

33

Going Home

I didn't know I was on my final approach back to church – and back to God – when I made the ninety minute drive to Karen's house.

I thought I was just going on a date.

Karen and I were supposed to meet a week later at a lunch with a mutual friend, Terries[i].

When Terries told Karen she wanted to get us together, one of Karen's first questions was, "Is he a Christian?"

Terries had answered, "Yes."

Karen was cautious, especially since she had a three year old son to consider. She asked for my phone number so she could check me out before we met.

I was cautious too, even though I had only myself to consider. I wasn't in the market for a relationship, not with a woman and certainly not with God. Neither had worked out well in the past. I asked for Karen's phone number so I could check her out before we met.

Karen called me at work one day.

We spoke briefly.

I called her at home that night.

We talked for eight hours.

In the course of that conversation we decided not to wait until our lunch with Terries. I would make the hour-and-a-half drive to Karen's

---

i. Real name.

165

house and meet her after church on the upcoming Sunday.

In the meantime, Karen called Terries. "I thought you said he was a Christian."

"He is," Terries replied. "He just doesn't know it yet."

Before I left that Sunday, I looked up the movie theater closest to Karen's house. Then I called and jotted down the showtimes of the movies I wanted to see.

This was not because Karen and I planned to go to the movies.

It was my backup plan. If I gave in to my hesitation and decided to bypass her house, I'd have something else to do.

The odds were about 50-50 when I left home.

Exit 80 was the Moment of Truth. I got off there for Karen's house, or I continued to Exit 77 and the movies.

I took Exit 80.

When I arrived in front of Karen's townhouse, some ambivalence remained. I parked down the street a ways. But I did eventually get out of the car.

My first in-person conversation with Karen occurred as I walked up to her door. She told me I had to move my car; all the spaces were assigned. I think she said "Hello" first, but I'm not sure. It was a strange and brief beginning.

It was enough to let me know that she was as beautiful as she had seemed on the phone.

Also unusual was my first conversation with her son, Philip, who would turn four the next week. After being introduced, he said, "You want a beer? Everybody else has one."

I had never dated anyone with a kid. If this was how it was going to be, it was going to be okay!

Karen said she still had on her church clothes and needed to change.

Church! Another reason for my hesitation.

She asked me to change a light bulb above her stairs while she got ready. I still don't know if that was some kind of test, but I passed in spite of my fear of heights.

I didn't pass the next test.

Philip asked me to make him a peanut butter and jelly sandwich. My Probation Officer experience with older kids hadn't given me many opportunities to make PB&J sandwiches the way a three-year-old would like. I did my best, smearing reasonable portions of grape jelly and creamy peanut butter on the white bread.

I handed him the finished product.

His verdict was swift. "Not enough stuff!"

Philip forgave the sandwich fail. He participated in my first date with Karen. Thanks to him, I experienced a new place – Discovery Zone, a kid-oriented maze of tunnels and ball pits with video games and pizza.

Not my usual first date. But fun.

And well worth the drive.

The tentative journey that almost wasn't turned out to be the first of many trips to Karen's townhouse. Never again did I make a backup plan for going past Exit 80.

But soon there was a catch.

34

Doing Time in the Big House (of God), Again

"I think I could fall in love with you."

That's what I said during hour seven or eight of the marathon phone call the week before I met Karen.

Yeah, it surprised me, too.

But soon something surprised me even more.

I knew Karen went to church every week. It was no surprise she wanted me to go with her. Not only was it important to her, she believed Philip needed the consistent example if I was going to be a regular part of his life.

Karen made her expectation clear: If I wanted to date her, I had to go to church with her.

You know how I felt about church and all the attendant religion stuff. But she only asked for an hour a week. That's all. One wasted hour; and not totally wasted because it would be spent with her.

What about my integrity? Wouldn't giving in make me a hypocrite, sitting there in church for perhaps the worst, most shallow reason ever? To keep a girlfriend?

Karen told me they had a softball team they'd let me play on.

I agreed to go.

I loved Sunday mornings before I met Karen. I'd sleep in, then stop by a convenience store and pick up a Washington Post. I'd hit a bakery for a sweet treat and a cup of coffee. For the rest of the morning I would linger over the paper, watch the Sunday morning news shows, and nap. When the weather was nice, I'd read and sleep in the hammock strung by the river that ran next to the farmhouse I rented.

Those were the days!

Now, it was almost like a sixth workday. I voluntarily got up early and put on decent clothes. Then I played church at Trinity Lutheran. I smiled at the usher when he gave me my bulletin. I greeted the good parishioners around me with a handshake during the Sharing of the Peace. I stood up and sat down and kneeled and stood up and sat down, following the pastor's direction for Lutheran Calisthenics. Sometimes I would even sing along with hymns I remembered from my childhood.

One thing I wouldn't do was go up for communion. That would have carried the charade too far.

At Karen's church, they celebrated communion every Sunday. The pastor's invitation to the altar for bread and wine carried the same winnowing words each week: "All baptized and believing Christians are welcome to come forward . . ."

With only 50% of the requirements satisfied, I remained in my pew while Karen went forward. At least I maintained a little of my integrity.

I had no idea what it meant to be Lutheran. I really didn't care.

I was just doing time.

Going to the Contemporary Service made the time go a little quicker. Listening to the praise band felt a lot less like church than the old-time majesty of the organ. Where else did you hear organs anymore, besides baseball games and *The Phantom of the Opera*?

Three pastors served at Trinity Lutheran. I paid more attention to their distinct preaching styles than the content of their sermons.

Pastor John Austin, the Senior Pastor, paced the chancel with energy and enthusiasm. Occasionally funny, always assured, he commanded attention like the top rooster in the pen. Pastor John had been the catalyst for the church's growth to over 2000 members.

Pastor Paul, John's son and the third generation of Austins to serve at Trinity, presented a more low-key pitch. He used lots of stories from his youth and related well to folks of all ages. Pastor Paul explained theological concepts like grace, repentance, and forgiveness, something that would be important to me later when I started paying attention.

Finally, Pastor Chuck's approach reflected his years in the corporate world. As he most likely did when he began a business presentation, he always started with a joke. I figured he got them from some book of humor for pastors. Despite the jokes, Pastor Chuck was more serious than the other two. I did appreciate the real-world experience he brought to his sermons.

Later, I would appreciate all three as excellent preachers.

And co-workers or bosses.

But that's getting way ahead of the story. Out there in the pew, I had no idea I'd ever be up front. No way did I think God was preparing *me* to preach by letting me hear three styles that would merge into my own delivery.

I wasn't even a Christian. I didn't want to be a Christian.

I just wanted to date Karen.

Karen just wanted me to go to church with her.

We both got more than we bargained for.

35

Emmaus, Finally

I can't tell you precisely when I fell in love with Karen. It was a process, not an event. It began on that marathon phone call, and continued through dates and quiet moments and nervous introductions to family and friends. The more time I spent with her, the more time I wanted to spend with her. The more I got to know her, the more about her I wanted to know.

"Falling" in love implies a gravitational pull. It's an autumn leaf drifting to the ground. Leaves don't drop in a straight line. They flutter and even hover, but the general and inevitable action is falling.

I did not make a decision to love Karen. It happened to me. She happened to me. My choice was not whether to love her or not, but what to do about it.

———

In order to germinate, seeds need water, oxygen, and the proper temperature. With the right conditions, they emerge from dormancy and begin to grow. Dormancy can last fifty years; scientists determined one germinating seed was at least 2000 years old.

I sat there in church week after week. My arms were crossed, figuratively if not always literally, in disinterest and dismissal.

But conditions were right for germination.

God's Word, read and preached, worked on me and in me. We Lutherans talk about God's Word as a Means of Grace, a vehicle for bringing God's unconditional, undeserved love to us.

I tried to ignore the Bible readings and sermons, but despite my intentions they warmed and watered the dormant seeds buried in my being over the previous thirty-three years.

The words for God's Spirit in both the Hebrew Scriptures (*ruah*) and in the New Testament's original Greek (*pneuma*) mean "wind" or "breath." The Holy Spirit breathed life into my dormant faith.

Faith was no more my decision than revival is for an unconscious recipient of CPR.

I could no more decide to believe the good news about Jesus than I could decide to fall in love with Karen.

If it had been my decision, based on what I thought I knew about following Jesus, I confess I would have decided against it.

I told you at the very beginning of our journey together there was no moment of epiphany. No flash of light or voice of God from the clouds.

I experienced not a revelation but a realization.

I realized Jesus was exactly who he claimed to be.

I realized I was a beloved child of God.

I realized I believed that stuff.

If you've ever seen *My Fair Lady*, you can read my reaction in the voice of Rex Harrison as Professor Henry Higgins when he realizes he has unintentionally "grown accustomed to her (Eliza's) face":

"Damn! Damn! Damn! DAMN!"

I did not make a decision. Belief happened to me. Jesus happened to me. My choice was not whether to believe or not, but what to do about it.

————

Eight months after we met, Karen and Philip visited a Family Camp Weekend for at-risk children and their families where Terries and I facilitated the adolescent group. At the first gathering of families on Friday night, I always did a goofy preview of the weekend's activities wearing a life jacket and a ropes course helmet. I held up a canoe paddle. "What's this?"

"A canoe paddle!" the families (especially the young children) would shout.

"This weekend we're going canoeing!" Then I'd repeat the process with a rope (ropes course!), a spatula (great food!), scissors (family crafts!), a CD (Saturday night dance party!) and so on. The last object

I held up was an old, holey hiking boot. Hikes!

This time there was a little twist. After the response, I put my hand in the boot and felt around. "There's something in here." I held up the small square box I took out of the boot. "What's this?"

"A box!"

I opened the box and pulled out the ring. "What is this?"

"A ring!" On what Philip eventually dubbed the Ring Video, you can hear the excitement as everyone has now figured out what is going on.

I knelt in front of Karen.

"Will you marry me?"

After she said, "Yes," I slipped the ring on her finger.

Then I turned to Philip. "Is it okay for me to be part of your family?"

He said, "Yes," too.

———

Karen and I met with Pastor John for our initial wedding planning meeting. We were relieved when he agreed to preside at our wedding at the camp rather than the church. I think Karen assumed there were more than sentimental reasons I preferred the camp. We hadn't talked much about my growing realization. I was still figuring it out. She didn't want to pressure me. Being wise and perceptive, she knew it would be counterproductive.

So when Pastor John asked if we wanted Communion to be part of our wedding service, she hesitated.

I answered immediately.

"Yes."

After all, Pastor John said week after week in worship that communion is for those who are baptized.

And believe.

The Unexpected
Pastor

36

Job and I Have Questions

"All you need is the faith of a mustard seed, Dave!"

When Pastor Paul invited my new member class to interrupt him any time we had questions, I took him literally – and liberally.

I had questions.

Lots of questions.

Over the six weekly class sessions, I tried to ask them all. I even drove over two hours each way from Atlantic City so I could attend the last class. My friend Mike had taken me there for three days the week before my wedding. The casino missed out on one evening of my contributions so I could ask my questions.

I don't remember what class it was, but Pastor Paul finally had enough.

His exasperated response about mustard seed faith shut my questions down.

For a few minutes.

I had my hand up so much I could've been mistaken for a Pentecostal.

A good deal of my identity has always been rooted in knowing the right answers. Or, on *Jeopardy!*, knowing the right questions.

Pastor Paul could not answer all my questions about God. No one could.

Most troubling, I could not know all the answers, or even all the questions.

Not knowing the answers is my personal hell.

Christian faith pursued honestly confirms the old canard, "The more you know, the more you know you don't know." That's especially true of an infinite God.

God is omniscient[i]. I'm not.

As I lived into my new faith, my list of questions only grew longer. What I didn't know about God, the Bible, and everything else kept me up at night. I badgered God for the answers as persistently as I had Pastor Paul.

Certainly God could handle my constant queries. But that didn't mean God would provide every answer.

It wasn't that my questions were unanswerable – God knows everything, after all – but God knew (and knows) that I didn't need to know everything. Many of the answers were more than I can handle.

As you might imagine, I had trouble accepting that.

I would not rest in what I did know, what I could know, and trust the rest would be revealed . . . or not.

I dwelled on why God didn't make this faith thing more obvious. Why require belief in someone who lived 2000 years ago, whose record of miracles and teaching – even death and resurrection – we can only apprehend through the murkiness of ancient history? Why not send someone now?

Sometimes on those sleep-deprived nights, as both body and mind tossed and turned, I felt like Judas in *Jesus Christ Superstar*, who wonders in the title song why Jesus didn't wait for mass communication.

"I only want to know," Judas sings at the end of that song.

"I only want to know." Story of my life.

That's the bottom line, my biggest obstacle to faith.

Knowledge is my idol.

"If I can just know enough . . ."

Then what?

The problem with a sticky brain like mine is buying into the illusion that you can think your way out of anything. When you've always

---

i. Omniscient is fancy church talk for all-knowing. Omnipotent means all-powerful. You can probably guess that omnipresent means everywhere at the same time. I will coin a new word, omnichronic, for the belief that God is present at every time simultaneously. That quality of God is subject to more debate than the others, but I love what C. S. Lewis said about a God who is outside of time – God therefore has an infinity to spend with each one of us.

perceived yourself as the Smartest Person in the Room (except the *Jeopardy! Tournament of Champions* Green Room), then you don't need anyone else. You don't need God.

You just need answers. The *right* answers.

I still struggle with this stuff.

The unanswered questions that still impinge on my sleep are more about me than about God. I insist God provide me with the answers, and I get pissed off when God doesn't.

————

Sometimes I picture God as Jack Nicholson on the witness stand in *A Few Good Men*, snarling at me, "You can't handle the truth!"

Not a pretty picture, but that's the God who shows up in a whirlwind in the book of Job.

When we meet him at the start of his eponymous book, Job is a faithful and rich dude with a large family. Before we're out of the first chapter, God makes a bet with Satan[ii] (seriously). Satan claims Job is only faithful to God because he's living the good life. God counters that Job would be faithful even if things weren't so great. God allows Satan to do anything he wants to Job as long as he doesn't hurt him physically.

Poor Job loses everything. Not only does all of his stuff get stolen or destroyed, all of his children and their families die.

Job grieves and laments, but he stays faithful.

Satan proposes a modification to the wager. He tells God that Job is only faithful because he's healthy. And if you have your health, you have everything. (Satan doesn't exactly say that, but you get the idea.)

So God says, "Go for it. Just don't kill him."

Poor Job gets sick. Terrible sores infest his body.

Job sits on an ash heap and scrapes at his itching, oozing skin with broken pottery. His wife tells him to curse God and die.

But still Job is faithful.

That doesn't mean he doesn't have questions. The big one is this: WHY?!

For almost forty chapters, Job's friends "comfort" him with their explanations. All their pontificating can be summed up like this:

————

ii. Job is sort of a parable. The character of Satan in the story is literally what his name means, "The Accuser," and not the fallen angel presiding over hell trying to tempt folks.

"Job, you must have done something really, really bad."

Job knows he doesn't deserve what has happened to him.

Of course Job doesn't know about the bet.

He demands an answer from God.

That's when God as Jack Nicholson on the witness stand shows up in a whirlwind.

God never answers Job's "Why" questions.

What God does – and this is one of my favorite passages of the Bible – is get sarcastic. "Yeah, Job, you can understand the mind of an infinite God. You were there when the world was created. You can make the sun rise and set. You can make it rain."

God points Job beyond himself to the vastness of creation, and to its living inhabitants.

> Where were you when I laid the earth's foundation?
> Tell me, if you understand.
> Who marked off its dimensions? Surely you know![iii]
>
> Can you bind the chain of the Pleiades?
> Can you loosen Orion's belt?
> Can you bring forth the constellations in their seasons
> or lead out the Bear with its cubs?
> Do you know the laws of the heavens?
> Can you set up God's dominion over the earth?[iv]
>
> Do you hunt the prey for the lioness
> and satisfy the hunger of the lions
> when they crouch in their dens
> or lie in wait in a thicket?
> Who provides food for the raven
> when its young cry out to God
> and wander about for lack of food?[v]

iii. Job 38:4-5a

iv. Job 38:31-33

v. Job 38: 39-41

The answer to God's questions is, "Not you, Job."

God reminds Job it's not all about him, and shows him a bigger picture beyond his suffering.

God implores Job to consider what God has made and what God keeps going. Considering all of that, Job must realize he would not comprehend the "Why" even if God were to answer him.

Job hoped knowing "Why?" would somehow lessen his suffering. God exposed this as false hope.

Instead of knowing "Why?" God invited Job to know God. Instead of knowledge, God offered Job . . . God.

That's what God offers me.

To become a Christian meant beginning the process of admitting I needed forgiveness and salvation and all that, but also that I needed to let go of my idolatry of knowledge.

By the way (SPOILER ALERT), Job gets back all of his stuff – and more! – at the end of the story. He gets a new family, too. The most remarkable thing, though, is that he asks God not to punish his friends even though they had spoken falsely about the nature of God.

And God does forgive them.

Grace abounds!

Job never does get his questions answered, though.

————

Like Job, I have, and will have, questions – lots of questions – that won't be answered. Not in this life anyway.

As I imagine eternity, there will be a Cosmic Question Booth somewhere on the fringes. The line will be long, but I'll wait.

I'll have forever, after all.

I don't believe as some do that we will know everything instantly in eternity. How much better will it be to continue learning... forever!

For now, in this life, I'm still learning to be comfortable with *not* knowing.

Not knowing is necessary for faith.

If I knew absolutely everything, if it all could be proved empirically and catalogued and tamed, then there would be no need for faith.

Faith is different than knowledge. They are not, however, mutually exclusive. Faith untethered from the real world is useless and may even be mental illness.

But what do you do – what do I do – when the real world seems to conflict with the world of faith? What about the apparent conflicts between science and belief in God?

37

Quantum God

A while back, I took a trip to the Maryland Zoo in Baltimore with my daughter and her friend. I have always enjoyed going to zoos, especially since they've been improved from the stark concrete cages in which animals were once confined. We saw an amazing variety of creatures. There were huge elephants, including a pachyderm giving itself a shower with its trunk, and tiny amphibians like the bright Panamanian Golden Frog. We saw birds and fish and reptiles from around the world, as well as my favorite animals: the always alert prairie dogs in their village of holes and tunnels.

As we walked around, I thought about some of the other zoos I've had the opportunity to visit, especially when I backpacked through Europe in the '80s. I realized how different the experience is for me now that I'm a Christian. Then, I looked in wonder at the animals in their beauty and variety. I still do. But now, something deeper and more wonderful happens. I am amazed not just by the creatures but by their Creator.

The Walters Art Museum is another place in Baltimore we like to visit. As we explore the gallery and linger over our favorite masterpieces by famous artists, I exclaim, "Look, a Raphael," or, "Wow, Monet!"

At the zoo, every animal is an opportunity to say, "Wow, God!"

Every mountain, seashore, desert, lake, and star-filled sky is an opportunity to say, "Wow, God!"

Has my pendulum of reason swung to the other extreme? Have I now rejected science and embraced the fundamentalist creation package of seven literal days of creation 5000 or so years ago?

If you've read this far, I hope you know me better than that.

I once thought that's what it meant to be a Christian. I thought when you entered a church you had to check your brain at the door.

When I realized I believed the stuff about God and Jesus, I feared it meant I had to give up science and reason.

I discovered that not to be the case.

Some churches do have a metaphorical Brain Check Booth as you enter, as questions, speculations and (especially) doubts are not welcome inside. Science is perceived as an enemy of faith.

It seems to me that questions, speculations and (especially) doubts are an inevitable part of faith that grows and matures.

Science only enhances my wonder at God's creativity and general awesomeness.

"In the beginning, God created," the first five words of the Bible, answers the "Who?" of creation. The rest of that first chapter – and indeed the rest of the Bible – is about "Who?" and as much "Why?" as we need to know.

"How?" is a question for science.

The conflict occurs when we confuse those questions. Folks look to that first chapter of Genesis for the "How?" of creation, as if astronomy and quantum physics would make sense to the Iron Age people God inspired to write it. The description of those days of creation is epic poetry, the art and beauty of which is desecrated when forced to function as a science textbook. That soaring, majestic account worships the Creator who is indeed the origin of everything.

Reading about astronomy and quantum physics, even though I don't understand it all, is also an act of worship.

When I learn about astronomy, I am reminded that God is the God of the unimaginably big.

If you can get to a place with no light pollution on a clear night, you might see 2000 or even 3000 stars.

That seems like a lot.

But there are over 200 *billion* stars in our own galaxy alone.

That seems like a lot.

A German computer recently estimated there are 500 billion *galaxies* in the universe. Astronomers estimate one *septillion* stars in the universe. That's a one with twenty-four zeros. That's more stars than grains of sand on all the beaches on the earth (750 quadrillion, which is 750 with "only" fifteen zeros).

That *is* a lot.

Can you imagine a God who created every one? A God who keeps track of every one?

I can't either. But to meditate on the God who operates on that scale is an act of worship.

God is the God of the unimaginably big.

God is also the God of the infinitesimally small.

Did you know there is gold in your body? Lots of gold, if you measure it in atoms. In a 180 pound human body, there are twenty *quintillion* atoms of gold. That's a twenty with eighteen zeros for those keeping score at home.

That sounds like a lot.

If you were to sell a gold dealer all the gold in your body at a rate of $1500 an ounce, you'd be rich, right? Not really. A generous gold dealer who rounded up would give you a penny.

Twenty quintillion atoms of gold weigh only .000008 ounces. Those atoms are pretty darn small.

Here's something else to think about. Your body is made up of more atoms than there are stars in the universe. Do you want the number? There are around

$$7,000,000,000,000,000,000,000,000,000[i]$$

atoms in your body, give or take a few if you just ate a cookie or sneezed.

Can you imagine a God who keeps track of all those atoms?

Neither can I.

But when my mind is blown by quantum physics, which is the science of the very, very, very small where the rules are different, and there is uncertainty and randomness, and some things seem to be both particles and waves at the same time, I am reminded God is the God of the infinitesimally small.

---

i. I'll save you the counting - that's twenty-seven zeroes, so seven octillion.

You and I are two of about seven billion people on the earth. Earth is a pretty nondescript planet in the outer corner of our galaxy, in the midst of hundreds of billions of other galaxies in the universe.

When we think about all those atoms and all those stars and all those people, we could feel pretty insignificant, couldn't we?

With God creating and keeping track of all that unimaginably big stuff and all that infinitesimally small stuff, how important could we individual human beings be?

How important could you be?

Psalm 139 says God knit you together in your mother's womb. God knit you together out of those seven octillion atoms.

That's why this science stuff doesn't lessen my appreciation or awe of God. I praise God all the more. Seven octillion atoms!

I am, in the words of that Psalm, "Fearfully and wonderfully made." And so are you.

———

That leads me to one more thing: I just quoted Psalm 139 which talks about God knitting people together in their mother's wombs.

I believe God creates each person. I do *not* believe God wields cosmic knitting needles to knit angel hair thread inside women's wombs. Neither do seven-literal-days-of-creation Christians. Those fundamentalists – and I – believe God creates through the natural processes of reproductive biology.

In the same way, I believe God created and continues to create – and recreate – everything that exists. God creates through natural processes, including (and I'm about to be condemned to hell by a certain subset of Christians) evolution.

I no more need to take literally the first chapter of Genesis than I do Psalm 139.

That's what I didn't understand when I was an unChristian.

Christians do not need to fear science as a threat to faith.

Science investigates questions about creation. To know more about creation means to know more about the Creator.

To know more about Monet's paintings is to know more about Monet.

Thanks to science, we know more and more about God.

———

Although scientific knowledge might enhance our faith, there's more to faith than knowing stuff.

Faith transcends knowledge. It might be described as a leap from knowing to something else, a leap across a chasm of the unknown to grab hold of something – Something Better – we hope is out there in the darkness.

Here's the amazing thing.

I never decided to make that leap. When hope opened me to the slimmest possibility of faith, God grabbed me while I wasn't looking and carried me across that chasm to the other side where, yes indeed, there was Something Better.

Someone Better, waiting with open arms. Someone who held on and did not let go.

Amazing Grace.

But that doesn't mean I'm always comfortable being held.

My self-worth had long been based on knowing the right answers and therefore not having to ask for help.

I needed to learn not just to ask for help, but to accept it.

I did, but it was painful. Literally.

38

A Crash Course

The gas gauge on my red Saturn SL-1[i] pointed right at the
E. I was still adjusting to the two-hour commute from Karen's town-
home, where I'd moved after we married a few months before. I hadn't
built time into that morning's schedule to stop for gas, and I had an
Intake Hearing with an alleged Juvenile Offender first thing. There
weren't any gas stations until I got to Centreville, the town where I
worked, anyway. In hindsight, it's probably a good thing there wasn't
a lot of gas in the car.

A little over halfway into the trip I neared one of the many flash-
ing-light intersections. I zoomed along at fifty-five miles per hour (or
so). A car approached from the right. I didn't pay much attention to
it. I was focused on the road – and the day – ahead.

I got almost to the intersection and only had time to think:

"He's not going to stop."

I jerked the wheel slightly to the right, just in time or we would've
T-boned.

Noise! Tires squeal, futilely grabbing pavement. Metal on metal
sound eruption then deeper compacting growl. Crash of windows
breaking. My voice, sharp profane outburst.

Then silence as the world went round and round.

No control.

---

i. You may remember Saturn as the car company with no-haggle pricing. Incidentally, that
car replaced the Toyota Tercel I was driving when I totaled three cars in the accident I mentioned earlier.

I had smashed into the larger vehicle's rear door on the driver's side. We whirled off the road together like pairs skaters locked in a synchronized spin.

When the cars came to rest in a ditch, I checked to make sure I had all my limbs. They were all accounted for, but dark liquid covered my right leg.

"Oh my God, I'm bleeding! Bleeding to death!"

It took me a few moments to realize I'd only been baptized by my half-cup of (fortunately) cold coffee.

Both cars were crumpled, accordion-style. Anybody driving by would've assumed serious injuries.

The other driver and I both emerged from our cars.

After making sure the other guy was okay, I wandered over to a little diner on the corner. Someone had already called 911; the folks inside convinced me to stop pacing and sit down. My heart raced and threatened to jump out of my body like *Alien*, but other than that I felt surprisingly good.

I got an ambulance ride and a clean x-ray at the emergency room. Karen picked me up and we stopped by my office on the way home.

"I'm taking the day off, " I told them. "See you all tomorrow."

Tomorrow turned out to be two months later.

That night I got out of bed and confirmed the theory of gravity, falling to the floor when my legs wouldn't hold me. I couldn't get back up.

What was happening?

I scrambled around like a roach on his back. Karen, awakened by the "thud," tried to help me back into bed. "I'll just sleep here on the floor," I finally declared so we could both get some rest.

A few doctors' appointments later, it was determined that every muscle in the right side of my back from my hip to my neck was in spasm.

I hurt so much the orthopedist prescribed morphine. Straight.

This isn't an addiction story, but eventually coming off the stuff was no fun. Knowing what we know now about opioids, I am thankful to have avoided dependency on the painkillers.

Weeks of physical therapy ensued. I needed not only the therapists and doctors, but rides to get there. Driving, especially our manual shift vehicles, was out of the question. I could slowly and painfully traverse short distances on my own, leaning on my dad's old shillelagh. Once I collapsed on the bed or the couch, I stayed put for a while. I needed help to get anything that wasn't in my reach.

I don't believe God caused that accident. But God used the results to teach me to lean on other people so I could ultimately learn to lean on God.

I learned more than that.

———

One Sunday Karen returned from church and told me Pastor Chuck wanted to visit.

I didn't feel like entertaining anyone. Small talk is never my strength, and small talk with a pastor couldn't be much fun.

I shook my head. "I don't think so."

"He just wants to pray with you. And give you communion since you haven't been able to get to church. That's what happens when you're a member of the congregation."

I don't remember if Karen had already told Pastor Chuck it was okay to stop by or if she convinced me first, but a couple days later he did appear at the door of our townhouse.

We talked for a while, then he opened up a little black case. It had little plastic cups and a small container of wine along with some of the tasteless communion wafers. He poured the wine and laid out a wafer. There was a short service of prayers and Scripture, then the Words of Institution.

The intimate celebration moved me more than I expected. I felt the gravity of the situation at the Last Supper in a way I hadn't before. "In the night in which he was betrayed..." I had never thought much about this communion thing starting on the night Jesus was handed over to be arrested, tortured and killed.

I had never thought much about Jesus instituting communion at a meal with people who would betray him, deny him, and run away later that same night.

People like me.

"The body of Christ, given for you," Pastor Chuck said as he handed me the wafer.

"The blood of Christ, shed for you."

A few years later, I would sit before a panel of clergy and lay folks who would determine my suitability to become a pastor. Bishop Jerry Knoche asked me, "How would you sum up what it means to be a Christian?"

"That's a good question," I responded. In addition to buying me a little time, it doesn't hurt to compliment the bishop. I paused and reflected for a moment.

I knew this one!

"For you."

"Those words we hear every time we receive communion. For *you*. Jesus' body and blood, for us. For me. It is so intimate, so personal. Every time I hear those words I'm reminded this faith is mine because it has been given to me."

The bishop must have liked my answer, because here I am wearing a clerical collar as I type this.

My love for those words, "For you," began in my living room with Pastor Chuck and his little communion kit.

After the sacrament, we talked about my faith journey and about some of my questions. Receiving communion opened me up – I'm sure the morphine didn't hurt, either.

I told Pastor Chuck I wanted to learn more. I had read some of the Bible during my convalescence and was frustrated by its opacity. I lacked background and experience.

A few days later, Pastor Chuck dropped off a commentary on the Gospel of John by twentieth century Scottish Bible scholar William Barclay.[ii]

There are two books besides the Bible that figured most prominently in my early growth as a Christian.

The first was C. S. Lewis' *Mere Christianity*, the book recommended by Dan in Vienna ten years before.

The commentary on John by Barclay was the second. I couldn't put it down! I had to buy Pastor Chuck another copy because I even read it during the long baths I took to soothe the pain. It just wasn't the

---

ii. Barclay's Daily Bible commentaries on the books of the New Testament are full of fascinating historical context and accessible theology. Some of that theology is controversial if not heretical (doubts about the Trinity, miracles, and hell); Braclay described himself as a "liberal evangelical."

same after I dropped it into the water a couple of times.

Reading Barclay's commentary recaptured the thrill I discovered in college learning about Shakespeare and other great literature. I had changed my major to English back then.

I didn't know it, but I was being prepared for another, even bigger, change.

39

The Unexpected Pastor

Lots of Lutheran pastors move through life undercover. Apart from worship leadership – and sometimes even then – they don't wear a clerical collar that identifies them as a religious leader. I understand the reasons for not wearing one. It can be off-putting, especially to folks who haven't been around churches much.

When I'm on pastoral duty, I almost always wear shirts with the white square tab at the base of my neck. That's mainly because I heard Pastor John say once, long before I was a pastor, "I don't take off the collar when I go to the store; you never know when someone there might need a pastor."

If I hadn't been wearing the collar, I probably wouldn't have had the discussion a while back with the Sandwich Artist[i] at Subway about how she drifted away from her faith and how she was feeling like she really needed a blessing right then. I wouldn't have had an encounter at the Wawa convenience store with the Assistant Manager who had a few things that were bothering him about the Bible. And I wouldn't have prayed with the grocery store checkout lady feeling overwhelmed with health and family issues.

The clerical collar has given me some great opportunities for ministry beyond the church, but there's another more immediate reason I often wear the pastor uniform:

I'm still so surprised I'm a pastor, I can use a reminder every time I

---

i. That's really what they're called.

look in a mirror.

"Wait, what?"

"Oh yeah."

This pastor gig was never my idea.

Like my return to faith, my journey to the pulpit unfolded gradually.

My hunger to learn more about the Bible and God, and my wonder at what I learned, continued undiminished after the effects of the accident – and the morphine – waned.

I took every Bible Study at church I could. I got involved in a Men's Small Group Bible Study that met weekly.

Lutheranism provided a whole new lens through which to view Christianity. Without knowing what *hermeneutic*[ii] meant, I developed a hermeneutic of grace.

Ephesians 2:8-9, so crucial to Luther and the Lutheran church, established the organizing principle for all the information I took in:

"For it is by grace you have been saved, through faith - and this is not from yourselves, it is the gift of God - not by works, so that no one can boast."

Grace toppled my carefully constructed tower of negative assumptions about Christianity – and about God. Those assumptions were formed and bolstered by misguided Christians themselves. But the truth – about grace, about unconditional love, about freedom – was there all along.

But because it was grace, it found me.

Much of my pursuit of knowledge was clandestine.

I read the Bible on my lunch hour at work. I didn't want anyone to think I was some kind of a Holy Roller, so I ate in my office with my door closed. "I've got some work I need to do over lunch," I'd say, rejecting the invitation to the lunchroom where I usually joined the gang before.

If I was out and about during the lunch hour, I'd get my food at a drive-thru, then eat in the parking lot. I balanced the Bible on the

---

ii. Hermeneutic is a lens through which to interpret the Bible. Everyone who reads the Bible processes the text through conscious and/or subconscious filters. Hermeneutics - the study of interpretation - attempts to define and utilize those lenses or filters. Even those who claim to read the Bible "literally" have their own hermeneutic.

steering wheel as I did my best not to get Taco Bell hot sauce all over my good clothes.

Speaking of seed planters, the Bible I was reading was a wedding gift from Doug.

The feeling – the certainty – that I was supposed to do something else started as a tickle but grew in intensity to something I couldn't ignore.

I discovered the next verse in Ephesians chapter two, which has since become my favorite verse of the over 30,000 in the Bible:

"For we are God's handiwork, created in Christ Jesus to do good works, which God prepared in advance for us to do."

What had God prepared in advance for me to do?

After recovering from the accident, I changed jobs and reduced my commute by two-thirds. My new position was Manager of Community Training for a child abuse prevention agency called The Family Tree. In the two years I was there, I designed and conducted over 250 parenting and child abuse recognition workshops in schools, community centers, and other locations primarily in inner-city Baltimore. I worked with groups as small as three, and spoke in front of audiences that filled school auditoriums.

All that public speaking was great preparation for something like preaching. But *me*, preaching?

That was hilarious!

But... I had been watching the pastors on Sundays, wondering about their training, thinking, "I could do that."

That was hilarious!

I started talking regularly with Pastor Chuck about what I was feeling. As a second career pastor himself, Pastor Chuck suggested that maybe, just maybe, I was experiencing a call to ministry.

That was hilarious!

But that was exactly what I had been thinking.

That was exactly what I had been fearing.

My Family Tree workshops were extremely successful both in the number of folks they reached and the evaluations filled out by the participants. I loved what I was doing. But I was dissatisfied. Something was missing.

It was hard to articulate, but as effective as the workshops were, I had to leave out what excited me the most. I could talk about reducing stress and methods of positive discipline and elements of effective communication with children, but I couldn't talk about God. Our organization was totally secular and most of the workshops took place in public schools, so religion was off-limits.[iii]

I helped parents find answers, but couldn't talk with them about The Answer.

The call to share The Answer became stronger.

That was hilarious!

But wait . . .

Something similar happened twice.

After one workshop, a woman walked up and said, "That was good, but it's not what you're supposed to be doing, is it?"

I asked her what she meant.

"I know the Spirit's upon you." She said she knew I would go into ministry.

Goosebumps.

After another workshop a few weeks later, a man approached me and said, "You can't keep it hidden. Where do you pastor?"

More goosebumps.

At the beginning of 1998, two years after marrying Karen and joining the church, Trinity decided to hire a Director of Christian Education. Karen was appointed to the Call Committee that would make the personnel decision.

Pastor Chuck told Pastor John that someone with lots of experience working with young people and families was thinking about getting more involved with the church.

One day I got a call from Pastor John. He wanted to meet with me. It was like being called to the principal's office. I wondered what I'd done!

Karen never intended to be part of a team interviewing her husband for a job. But she did. God had aligned everything just right.

I now had two jobs, which was great because we had a brand new daughter and Karen took an eighteen-month leave of absence from work, reducing our income significantly.

---

iii. As it should have been.

God had "prepared in advance," all right.

Pastor John modified the position responsibilities to include some pastor things like visitation of homebound and sick folks. Soon I was praying with people, like Pastor Chuck had done with me.

More and more people started asking when I was going to start seminary.

That was hilarious!

Pastor Chuck encouraged me to take a class or two at an ecumenical seminary in Baltimore where he'd started before he transferred to the Lutheran Seminary. They offered classes at night so I wouldn't have to miss work.

It turned out that ecumenical seminary was on the same road as my office.

In one of our discussions, Pastor Chuck made a suggestion. He said, "Why not try one course? You don't need to commit to a full load or to the candidacy process or anything like that – just see how it goes."

Then he said something really wise. "If you don't end up becoming a pastor, then the worst thing that will happen is you'll know more about God. And, since God is love, you'll realize even more how much God loves you."

"Just take one class."

He was like that guy at a party. "Just try one. One won't hurt you . . ."

———

I remember the first night of that one course. I found the classroom in an imposing gothic structure that was a Roman Catholic seminary by day and the Ecumenical Institute of Theology in the evening. Like I had in New Member Class, I sat right up front.

Very rarely in my life have I felt so sure I was right where I was supposed to be.

I aced that class (have to keep up my Too Smart cred), and then another. Eventually I transferred to the Lutheran Seminary in Gettysburg, but remained part time. I made the two-hour-each-way commute two or three days a week.

It took me nine years, but in May, 2007, I graduated with a Master of Divinity Degree. That's a ridiculous name for a degree, by the way. If there's one thing a person can never master, it's divinity.

On June 2nd, 2007, I was ordained and installed as an Associate Pastor at Trinity.

Goosebumps.

Still.

(And hilarious!)

———

Thank you, Cleopas, for taking this journey with me. Blessings on your journey!

Epilogue

Easter Promises for Mom

"It will be soon," the doctor said.

"Soon as in days or soon as in hours?"

"Hours."

I had twenty minutes alone with my mom. She lay in bed, under the covers except for her head. She was unresponsive.

Everything I'd heard, read, and experienced about the end of life indicates hearing is the last sense to go.

What could I possibly say that would encapsulate the forty-eight years we had known each other, especially the good chunk of time in the beginning when she took care of me, taught me, baked me cookies, patched me up when I was cut or bruised, and most of all just let me know I was loved?

Many of you reading this have experienced this difficult time with a loved one, perhaps quite recently. These are painful yet precious, even holy, moments.

For me, there were a myriad of emotions that day in the hospice room with my mom. Of course I grieved. I felt frustration at my inability to change the inevitable outcome. Anger also rose up in me, anger that my mom was only seventy-two and the last ten years of her life were stolen by Alzheimer's.

Even before this pitiful end, her very being, all of what made her "mom" – even her memory of her son and daughter and grandchildren – had been desecrated by Alzheimer's.

Fear mingled with my other emotions. It differed from the fear I experienced twenty-four years before when Dad died. Then, I didn't believe in salvation or in any kind of afterlife. When you were dead you were dead. I remember being afraid not so much of death, but terrified I would never see my dad again. I was dismayed by the finality of a forever farewell.

The fear I felt with Mom had more to do with her comfort, and also with my doing and saying the "right" things.

I confess, in my pastor role I am always intimidated and somewhat afraid at the bedside of a dying person. It is part of what I am called to do, and I am supposed to know what I am doing. When I accompany a family in that situation, I do my best to be led by the Holy Spirit. I know, however, that the Spirit's leading is filtered through all my imperfection. Whatever I do, it feels inadequate.

I feel inadequate.

And this was my *mom*.

I held her hand.

I talked to her about the things she had done for me.

I told her again I was able to work with kids and families in trouble before I was a pastor because of the great job she and Dad did raising Anne and me.

I told her the faith foundation they laid when we were growing up enabled me to answer God's unexpected call to ministry.

I thanked her again for the last time for all the stuff she did with Anne and me when we were little – the crafts at the kitchen table, the brownie batter bowls I licked, the stories she read to us, the "Woodman Terrace" song we sang on the front steps of the house on Gardenia Drive.

I told her again for the last time that the only reason I did well on *Who Wants to Be a Millionaire* and *Jeopardy!* was because of the curiosity and wonder about the world she instilled in me from the time I was very young. I thanked her for all the trips to the library, and for talking Dad into buying our set of *World Book Encyclopedias*.

Then we were just quiet for a while together.

The signs of mom's imminent death intensified. The purple in her feet and hands deepened and crept toward her ankles and wrists. The rise and fall of her chest became almost imperceptible. Labored breaths came after increasing pauses.

My fear intensified. I became frantic, pressured by the brief time remaining and sure I had not said enough.

I always feel inadequate.

Then . . .

I grabbed my Kindle and opened up one of my Bibles. I turned to the 28th Chapter of Matthew.

I read aloud the words of the Easter Gospel.

I read it for her.

I read it for me.

We came to verse five. "But the angel said to the woman, 'Do not be afraid; I know that you are looking for Jesus who has been crucified. He is not here, for he has been raised as he said.'"

"Do not be afraid. He is not here for he has been raised!"

The resurrection of Jesus Christ is not just a nice story we tell each other every year on Easter. It is not some allegorical myth or some mystical symbol. It is not even just Jesus' story.

It is *our* story.

The resurrection story is at the core of our faith and of our hope. It is the very core of our identity.

We are Easter People!

When I finished reading, the dark emotions still lurked within me, but joy and awesome wonder leavened my being. I felt the presence of God in that room. I knew God would never let go of her, that the promises God made to her in baptism held her not just in this life, but forever.

I knew my mom would not be cured. I knew she would die in a very short time.

But I also knew my mom would be healed, perfectly healed in a resurrection prefigured when Jesus walked out of his tomb on that very first Easter Sunday.

In the ultimate resurrection there will be no more Alzheimer's or any kind of sickness or sadness or even death. There will only be joy at the greatest family reunion ever.

The Happy Little Simpsons will be reunited for all eternity in the very presence of God. Amen.

Awknowledgements

Having written a book is awesome.
Writing a book is arduous.

Thank you to everyone who encouraged me to stick with it, and who told me they would read it and share it with others (it's put up or shut up time for you, by the way).

Thank you to the people of the congregations I have served as pastor:
Trinity Evangelical Lutheran Church in Joppa, Maryland;
Christ Evangelical Lutheran Church in Millersville, Maryland;
Good Shepherd Evangelical Lutheran Church in Frederick, Maryland;
and my internship congregation, St. John's Lutheran Church in
    Parkville, Maryland.
The Holy Spirit has worked through you to shape me into the pastor I am today (Credit? Blame? YMMV[i].)
Pastor Chuck Lashley at Trinity once told me that a pastor's primary job is to love the people of their congregation. I hope that you experienced the love I have for you as I ministered to you and with you – for I have felt loved by you.

Thank you to all the Seed Planters. Keep planting; I hope this book demonstrates that what might seem stony soil at first might prove to be fertile.

---

i. Yep, footnotes even in the acknowledgements. By now, you shouldn't be surprised. YMMV stands for "Your Mileage May Vary," a tagline from car commercials and now an online acknowledgement that your opinion may be different than that of others.

Thank you to everyone who has ever liked a post on Facebook that said I was writing a book or finishing a book or getting it published. Your clicks on the "like" or "love" icons helped keep me going.

Thank you to those who read the pre-edited version of the book and offered their encouragement and suggestions: my sister Anne, sister-in-law Diana, Scott Luthcke, and John Auger.

Thank you to Cindy Van Vliet, whose close proofreading I especially appreciate.

Thank you to the Corbin/Fontz/Gardner family for providing a beautiful place with the separation I needed to start writing this book.

Thank you to Diane Nine for your encouragement, faith, and work on behalf of this book.

Thank you to Brian Scott and 9 Foot Voice Publishing, for your belief in this book and your diligence to make it better. You gave me courage to excise parts of the book that needed to go. Thank you also for your patience as I juggled the various parts of my life.

Thank you to my children, Philip and Autumn, who inspire me and have given me my most valued title: Dad.

And thank you to Karen, my wife, my best friend, my most honest reader, who inspires me with her passion and bravery and commitment to positive change. I love you and am glad not only that you agreed to date me, but that we keep on dating now and into the future.

Soli Deo gloria![ii]

---

ii. Glory to God alone! Bach and Handel used to write "S.D.G" at the end of some of their compositions. It is one of the five great *solas* of the Protestant Reformation, along with *sola gratia* (grace alone), *sola fide* (faith alone), *solo Christo* (Christ alone), and *sola Scriptura* (Scripture alone). And that, dear reader, is the last footnote.

Made in the USA
Coppell, TX
20 April 2021